Border Voices /11

A BOOK OF POETRY BY SAN DIEGO STUDENTS AND INTERNATIONALLY ACCLAIMED WRITERS

ISBN, BORDER VOICES
0-9719906-2-X

Jack Webb
P.O. Box 120191
San Diego, CA 92112-0191

Professional and student poets featured in this anthology also read their poems at the 2004 Border Voices Poetry Fair. The Fair was presented by San Diego State University and *The San Diego Union-Tribune*

Art Director: Leslie L.J. Reilly
Lilac Design Studio

Editors: Chris Dickerson and Celia Sigmon

Biographies of featured poets: Jack Webb

Poet photos, page 15 — Adrienne Rich: Lilian Kemp; Robert Creeley: *Sunday Star*, Aukland, New Zealand, 1995, and New Directions; Sandra Cisneros: Rubén Guzman; Ken Waldman: Kate Salisbury.

Cover Illustrations: "Larry the Scary Ghost Kid" by Christian Ray Preston Rubio / Las Palmas Elementary; "Enigma" by Dan Driver / Standley Middle.

Table of Contents

Major Poets

Student Poets

SUN, MOON AND STARS

"Sunrise" by Hieu Phan / Morse High

NATURE'S TURN

"Black Cat" by Jethro Ancheta / Morse High

Rites of Passage

LOVE AND HATE

FOOD FOR THOUGHT

Honorable Mentions / 185

"Sweet Fire" by Hector Licon / Southwest Middle

Dedication

"Shooting Gleaming Star" by Anthony Corona
Las Palmas Elementary

This book is dedicated to the young artists among us – to those who lay their hands on the world as if for the first time, as if they were the first men or women, and tell us of the things they see, and dream, and love.

"For the creator must be a world for himself, and find everything within himself, and in Nature to which he has attached himself."

— Rainer Maria Rilke
Letters to a Young Poet

Introduction

BEYOND ELOQUENCE

By Jack Webb

"Dancing Spirit" by Kristina Kostenkova / Standley Middle

It was an overstressed day, a day that had my eyes blinking and watering as if I were slogging my way through a high wind, my brain shivering like a dandelion in a storm, neurons flying.

It was a typical day with Border Voices, full of kids and poems and TV shows, all of it part of the run-up to the glorious little book you hold in your hand. I'll share parts of that day with you in a minute, glittering vignettes that demonstrate how the Border Voices Poetry Project is more than the sum of its parts, more than poetry workshops for students and music-studded poetry fairs featuring celebrity writers: it is a series of eye-popping discoveries framed by smiles on children's faces.

But first, a little background, a heaping helping of context and justification and hope:

For the last 10-plus years, Border Voices has been sending 19 poets into schools throughout San Diego County, a sort of poetic roll-of-the-dice in the effort to promote both literacy and self-understanding among our young people. The results have been dramatic, as parents wrote that the workshops had "transformed not only our daughter, but our whole family," and grateful teachers raved: "You have ignited a series of Roman candles! These young people are writing, writing, writing!"

Awards flowed in – from the California Association of Teachers of English, from the Greater San Diego Reading Association, from San Diego City Schools. Money flowed in, from the National Endowment for the Arts, the San Diego Commission for Arts and Culture, the California Arts Council.

Every year we brought famous poets from around the world to our annual Poetry Fair, so that our students could rub shoulders and minds with some of the best writers of our time. Every year these poet laureates and Pulitzer Prize winners declared they'd never seen anything like what we'd created here.

But something was missing. Though kids and teachers told us that Border Voices had added something wonderful to their classrooms and lives, we had no hard proof that the project had actually accomplished anything in the battle for literacy. Our many volunteers had spent hundreds of hours on a dream, but dreams are hard to document. We feared that there was no Euclidean proof that we were really accomplishing anything of lasting value.

Until now.

Thanks to a $20,000 grant from the California Arts Council, we were able to hold a series of intensive poetry workshops in every classroom at Pershing Middle School in Spring 2002, with pre- and follow-up testing of the students. The principal, Sarah Sullivan, reported "huge and continuing increases in scores on standardized English tests" even after the intensive school-wide workshops ended, and even among students who entered the school after Spring 2002. She attributed the continuing increases, in part, to teachers adopting Border Voices methods of presenting creative writing, and she also said the workshops resulted in a new collegiality among the faculty and a campus-wide "educational Renaissance."

This is good stuff. Even better is the following table, which shows how the beneficial effects of Border Voices affected the entire student body:

ALL PERSHING STUDENTS, SPRING 2001-2003
Percentage of School's Students at Each Performance Level

English Language Arts

	Far Below Basic		Below Basic		Basic		Proficient		Advanced	
	#	%	#	%	#	%	#	%	#	%
2003	84	8.7	132	13.7	320	33.3	305	31.7	120	12.5
2002	92	10.0	152	16.5	338	36.8	256	27.9	81	8.8
2001	93	10.0	151	16.2	352	37.7	259	27.8	78	8.4

Note how the number of students performing at advanced levels on the test increased from 8.4 % of the student body before the workshops to 12.5 % afterward. Note a corresponding drop in those scoring below basic, or far below basic. School administrators credit Border Voices with providing the initial spark as well as continuing inspiration for this improvement.

We rejoice. And unlike T.S. Eliot – who had to "construct something / Upon which to rejoice" – we really DO have something to be happy about.

* * *

If you like, now's a good time to start leafing through this book, admiring the kids' poems and artwork. Or

"Lady of the Sun" by Kimberly Keith / Morse High

you can take five minutes to follow me through one day with Border Voices, through that blizzard/storm/steady drizzle of stimulation that I referred to in the first paragraph of this introduction. Your choice – fun either way.

* * *

I am writing this sentence at 5 a.m. the morning of Feb. 25, two months before our annual Poetry Fair. Less than a week ago, at 9 a.m., I was sitting on a stool in the studios of Instructional TV, a light brighter than the sun splashing the right side of my face, a teleprompter and a cold-eyed TV lens eight feet in front of me. The cameraman raised his hand, the teleprompter began to scroll its text. Braced by four expressos, hair combed, face made up, I began:

" . . . each aspiring young artist must begin again, from the beginning, must lay his hands on the world as if it were being done for the first time . . . I am delighted to present Robert Creeley – a man who found the courage to listen to his own heart."

I was filming the introductions to our annual TV series featuring the famous poets who were coming to the fair. The actual interviews with the poets wouldn't be conducted until April 23, but Richard Harrison – the deceptively happy-go-lucky director of ITV – liked to get housekeeping chores like the introductions done well in advance.

*"Life" by Libni Lam
Southwest Middle*

As I blinked sleepily and affectionately at the camera, I remembered the first time I'd gone on TV. The camera had petrified me. All those millions of eyes. Was my hair straight? Was my mouth twitching from nervousness? Oh, my good Lord – did I really pronounce "sonorous" as so-NOT-rous?

My nervousness lasted through the first two or three times I appeared on camera. Then I remembered two things:

1/ The great Shakespearean actor Richard Burton once told Johnny Carson that he always, invariably, would flub a line when reading "Hamlet." He did it deliberately because, he maintained, it aroused the audience's attention and sympathy. Thus, I didn't have to worry if I flubbed the word "sonorous" – I was following in the footsteps of the great Richard Burton.

2/ Martin Sheen told another interviewer about the lesson in acting he received from Marlon Brando. It was near the end of "Apocalypse Now," when Sheen was supposed to creep into the room of the demented and murderous colonel (Brando) while he was sleeping, brood over the snoring Brando, and then "terminate him with extreme prejudice." Sheen didn't know how to act the scene, and he botched take after take. Finally Brando opened his eyes and looked at Sheen. "Pray for the father," Brando said, in that dramatic throaty whisper for which he's famous. A startled Sheen thought about it for five seconds – and then played the scene to perfection. He had been reminded of something that all great actors know – that when you appear before the camera, you do not talk to the camera or even to your fellow actors in their own persona. You talk to someone you know, and you tell them things that are of great interest to them.

Thus, as I sat in the studios that morning, I was talking not to the camera, but to a friend of mine who was deeply interested in poetry. We had a good conversation. (P.S. – Two of the featured poets at the Poetry Fair agreed to appear on our TV show. You can read a modified form of the TV introductions I wrote for them in this book, in the brief biographies printed with the poems of Robert Creeley and Ken Waldman).

12:30 p.m. the same day – I am in Lori Moore's class at Franklin Elementary, just finishing up a workshop in poetry for some 5th graders. The kids are crowded around me, asking for my autograph. Five of them – those brave enough to read their newly crafted poems in front of the class – had received Border Voices anthologies as prizes, and I signed those. Others had me sign slips of paper, even collections of short stories by other authors. I remembered something the poet Gary Soto had told me with a sheepish grin when he'd been mobbed by kids who'd read his children's books: "My fans," he said. "Ain't it somethin'?"

One little girl handed me the book she'd won, and looked up at me with bright eyes. She was the one who'd written a really surprising poem, perfect ballad measure with exquisitely funny rhymes, in which she'd talked about her dream to get rich, buy a limousine, marry a cute husband "and we'd both eat some beans."

I looked at her, and then wrote in her book: "May you always keep the dreams in your eyes."

(NOTE: I'd treated the class to one of my best lesson plans, one that helped them learn to put magic in their writing. We'd laughed

our way through it, with kids popping up out of their seats as they thought of really good lines, and rushing over to share them with me. The "magic and poetry" lesson plan, if you're interested, is at the end of this introduction).

1:30 p.m., still that same day – Back at the TV studios with Sarah Sullivan, principal of Pershing Middle. We're watching student Jim Raney on the stool in front of the camera, reading his poem about his father's guitar. Jim is a good-looking young man, but he's stiff with uncertainty. The director, Harrison, has done take after take, and still isn't satisfied. Finally I say (thinking of Brando):

"Pretend you're talking to your girlfriend."

"He's only in middle school," Sarah whispers.

"Well, pretend you're talking to your best friend," I say.

"Yes, try that," Harrison says.

Jim Raney gets it right in one more take. We all clap and cheer.

* * *

All the other Border Voices volunteers could offer similar stories, and that's the point. Out of this maelstrom of community service a shared creativity has been born, and it has rebounded to our good, and to the good of our children.

I invite you now to sit back and relax with this book. When you're done, you can get this year's companion anthology, "Songs of Their Spirit, Songs of Their Joy: Poems by Tijuana Youth," which was produced from workshops we held at institutions for disadvantaged kids south of the border.

I suspect that, after reading the children's poems, you too will rejoice.

A Border Voices Lesson Plan:
Magic and Poetry

> *"You see there are in our countries rivers which have no names, trees which nobody knows, and birds which nobody has described . . . Our duty, then, as we understand it, is to express what is unheard of."*
>
> — Pablo Neruda

There are many different ways of approaching poetry, but they all have one thing in common – they are methods by which the poet can "kick-start" his or her imagination, forcing it to break out of conventional or learned ways of thinking and writing. One such technique is "magic realism," in which the poet introduces myths, ghosts and dreams into the reality of his life. Also called *lo real marvilloso*, or the mar-

"Cloudy Cloudy Life" by Lauren Miller / Standley Middle

velous real, this technique is especially appealing to younger students, but also exciting for older students as well as adults.

At the beginning of the class, I give the students a few examples of poems that have an element of magic. I also talk about how the human voice is the greatest of all musical instruments, and that if they learn to use it well, it will serve them well. If they wish to be lawyers, they will be more persuasive lawyers if they become adept at "playing" the rhythms of their voices. If they wish to be writers . . . or dancers . . . or actresses . . . they also have something to learn from this class.

"And how many of you would like to be rich?" I ask. Almost all the students raise their hands. "You can learn something here that will help you with that," I say. "There's money in poetry.

I paid Maya Angelou $35,000 to appear at one of our Poetry Fairs, $35,000 for an hour's work." The kids rustle in their chairs with astonishment.

"Now it's time to write your own magic realism poem. We'll take it step by step." I then proceed as follows, pausing after each step to give them a chance to write:

> **1/** Think of something you really want, something that is difficult or perhaps even impossible to achieve. Maybe you want to get an "A" on that oh-so-difficult history or math test, or perhaps someone close to you is ill and you would like to see them get well quickly. Maybe there is a pet you'd really like, a thoroughbred horse or a rare Tibetan dog, that you or your parents can't afford. Take a minute or two and write what you would like to have, preferably in one sentence.

> **2/** In one sentence, give a physical description of yourself. Are you bald? (LAUGHTER) Do you wear jewelry? Is your skin tanned or light, do you wear tattoos like Dennis Rodman? (MORE LAUGHTER) Be as accurate and vivid as possible.

> **3/** If the poem is about someone else, and what you would like for them, then write a physical description of the beneficiary of your magic-wish poem. Do they have eyes like walnuts, hair curved like a seashell? Find two or three things about them that are really "them," so that we would recognize them if we saw them in a crowd. "Oh yes, there's the tattooed lady with the seashell hair."

> **4/** Now imagine yourself (or the subject of the poem) trying to do the impossible thing, and failing. Describe what that's like, again in one or two sentences.

> **5/** Now imagine something magical that would let you achieve the thing you want. Perhaps it's an elixir that will turn you into a genius for a day, so you can write that history paper in a way that will wow your teacher.

Perhaps it's a mysterious billfold you find on the street, with one dollar in it; but when you pull the dollar out, another dollar magically appears in its place, and this continues until you have a huge pile of bills at your feet. In one or two sentences, describe the magical object, what it looks like, what it does.

6/ Again, in one or two sentences, describe what happens when you use the magical object to achieve your desires. You get exactly what you want – how does it make you feel? Are you happy? A little disappointed? Are there unexpected side-effects (your seashell hair turns blue, for example)?

7/ Now write down all those sentences as one poem. Feel free to juggle the words and lines around. When you're done, hand the poem to a classmate and let him look it over and make suggestions. You, of course, will be doing the same with his or her poem. Use any of the suggestions that feel "right" to you.

"Fairy in the Darkness" by Anna Lee / Standley Middle

Acknowledgements

"My Goal" by Sam Hoeck / Canyon View Elementary

This book and the April 2004 Poetry Fair are the result of a collaboration between dozens of poets, teachers and organizations; special thanks go to those organizations and individuals who helped underwrite this book and the Fair. Among those who have supported Border Voices with both donations and encouragement over the years are the James S. Copley Foundation; the National Endowment for the Arts; the John R. and Jane F. Adams Endowment; the California Arts Council; Deborah Szekely, president of the Eureka Communities foundation; the Fieldstone Foundation; Audrey Geisel of the Dr. Seuss Foundation; Poets & Writers, Inc; and the San Diego Commission for Arts and Culture. A special debt is owed the coterie of volunteer administrators who kept everything running smoothly through hard work leavened with humor, and especially the members of the executive board – Chris Baron, who doubled as fair manager; David Clary; Veronica Cunningham; Sylvia Levinson; and Celia Sigmon, who co-edited the annual anthology with Chris Dickerson. A respectful tip of the hat as well to Bonnie Miller, Randi Reyes and Louise Fuller, who assisted the anthology editors. Thanks also to the judges who selected the student art and poetry for this anthology, Chris Dickerson, Chris Fell, and Sylvia Levinson; and to the nationally recognized poets who helped select the winners in the annual Border Voices poetry contest: Robert Creeley and Ken Waldman, whose biographies and poems are featured later in this book.

And a VERY special thanks to *The San Diego Union-Tribune* for agreeing to co-sponsor the project, and to publish student poems and artwork in the newspaper at the time of the fair. Members of the *Union-Tribune* staff also have donated many hours of their own time to the project, which includes the bimonthly, countywide poetry contest Doorways to Vision launched in 2003.

Following is a list of others who have contributed money, in-kind contributions, or moral support to the Border Voices Poetry Project:

The Administrators Association of San Diego City Schools; the Associated Students of San Diego State University; the Association of San

Diego Educators of the Gifted; Claudia Axel; Barnes & Noble/Bookstar; Borders Books & Music; Francisco Bustos, who edited the Border Voices anthology "Songs of Their Spirit, Songs of Their Joy: Poems by Tijuana Youth"; California Poets in the Schools; Brandon Cesmat; the San Diego Chargers; the San Diego County Office of Education, with special thanks to Dr. Rudy M. Castruita, superintendent, and Richard A. Harrison.

Thanks also to Beverly Cramb, who spearheaded the introduction of Border Voices workshops in Tijuana orphanages; Glover Davis, co-director of the Master of Fine Arts Program in Creative Writing at San Diego State University; Jeri Denniston, community relations manager for the *Union-Tribune*; Doug Dickerson; Julia Doughty; Glory Foster; Kermeen Fristrom; Steve Garber; Jana Gardner; César González-T., founding chair of Chicano Studies at Mesa College; the Greater San Diego Council of Teachers of English; minerva (Gail Hawkins); Georgette James; Paula Jones; Roxanne Young Kilbourne; the vivacious and ever-helpful Susan Schiele, general book buyer and book event coordinator, SDSU Bookstore; Hope Meek; Jim Milner, former board member, excellent poet, and all-round good guy; Joe Milosch; Joan Marchese; Andres Monreal; Jill Moses and Johnnierenee Nia Nelson, co-area coordinatiors for California Poets in the Schools; Sherri Pineda, community relations representative for the *Union-Tribune*; Leroy Quintana of Mesa College; Margo Raynes of the *Union-Tribune*, who devoted many hours to the project; Leslie L.J. Reilly, the graphic artist who designed this book, the fair poster, and other odds and ends, astonishing everyone for yet another year with her brilliance and good humor; Border Voices intern Elsie Rivas; the San Diego Padres; Drew Schlosberg, community and public relations manager for the *Union-Tribune*; Joan Schlossman, for her unfailing support; Dr. Paul Wong, Dean of the College of Arts and Letters, SDSU; Gabriella Anaya Valdapena; and Karin Winner, editor, and Laura Wolfe, senior customer service representative, *Union-Tribune*.

Special thanks, too, to the San Diego Unified School District and its talented administrators and staff, including Alan D. Bersin, superintendent; Mary Hopper, chief academic officer, Office of Instructional Support; Debbie Beldoc, executive director, curriculum and instruction; Donna Marriott, assistant director, literacy and social studies; and the school board. We also owe thanks and gratitude to Sarah Sullivan, principal of Pershing Middle School, who helped the Border Voices Poetry Project organize and document one of its most ambitious programs – intensive poetry workshops at the school involving every student. And finally, sincere appreciation goes to the National School District and its staff, teachers and administrators for their many years of active involvement in the project.

Major Poets

ADRIENNE RICH

ROBERT CREELEY

SANDRA CISNEROS

KEN WALDMAN

"Enigma" by Dan Driver / Standley Middle

15

Adrienne Rich

Adrienne Rich is one of this country's most distinguished poets. Her poetry is taught in English and women's studies courses across the country, and she is a revered teacher and activist. Since receiving the Yale Younger Poets Award in 1951, at the age of 21, she has not stopped writing in her distinctive voice, and in a language that incites action and provokes deliberation – about poverty, racism, sexism, violence, love between women, problems of survival, isolation and marginality.

Rich is the recipient of numerous awards and honors: the 1999 Lannan Foundation Lifetime Achievement Award; the Ruth Lilly Poetry Prize; the Common Wealth Award in Literature; the National Book Award; the 1996 Tanning Award for Mastery in the Art of Poetry (the Wallace Stevens Award); and the MacArthur Fellowship. In 2003, she was awarded the Bollingen Prize for Poetry.

She is the author of 15 volumes of poetry, including *Diving into the Wreck*; *The Dream of a Common Language*; and *The Fact of a Doorframe: Selected Poems 1950-2001*. She has also authored four books of non-fiction prose, including *What is Found There: Notebooks on Poetry and Politics* (updated edition Fall 2003). Her most recent book of essays is entitled *Arts of the Possible: Essays and Conversations*. Her most recent collection of poems was published in Fall 2001 by W.W. Norton and is entitled *Fox*.

MESSAGES

I love the infinity of these silent spaces
Darkblue shot with deathrays but only a short distance
Keep of course water and batteries, antibiotics
Always look at California for the last time

We weren't birds, were we, to flutter past each other
But what were we meant to do, standing or lying down
Together on the bare slope where we were driven
The most personal feelings become historical

Keep your hands knotted deep inside your sweater
While the instruments of force are more credible than beauty
Inside a glass paperweight dust swirls and settles (Manzanar)
Where was the beauty anyway when we shouldered past each
    other

Where is it now in the hollow lounge
Of the grounded airline where the cameras
For the desouling project are being handed out
Each of us instructed to shoot the others naked

If you want to feel the true time of our universe
Put your hands over mine on the stainless pelvic rudder
No, here (sometimes the most impassive ones will shudder)
The infinity of these spaces comforts me
Simple textures falling open like a sweater

— Adrienne Rich

"Messages" from *Fox: Poems 1998-2000* by Adrienne Rich. Copyright © 2001 by Adrienne Rich.
Used by permission of the author and W.W. Norton & Company, Inc.
NOTE: Blaise Pascal (1623-1662): *Le silence éternel de ces espaces m'affraye*. (The eternal silence of
these infinite spaces frightens me). See *Pensées of Blaise Pascal*, trans. W.F. Trotter, Everyman's Library
no. 874 (London: Dent, 1948), p. 61.

EDITOR'S NOTE: The following was originally written as the introduction to a televised interview with Robert Creeley on the Border Voices TV show. It is presented here, with only slight changes and additions, as part of the educational mission of Border Voices, which delights in surprising juxtapositions and occasional epiphanies. The reader might compare this free-wheeling examination of Robert Creeley's work to the more traditional biographies of Adrienne Rich and Sandra Cisneros on adjoining pages.

Robert Creeley

Over the past few decades, Robert Creeley has been praised – and perhaps praised to excess – as "the essence of American poetry," "the primo levitator," and "the tender ember . . . (that's) kept invention alive" in American poetry. All this may or may not be true (though I'm sure Creeley's ears are burning as he listens to this introduction). What is indisputably true, however, is that Creeley is a man who learned in his 20s what every true artist needs to know – that each aspiring young artist must begin again, from the beginning, must lay his hands on the world as if it were being done for the first time. He or she must, as the great German-language poet Rainer Maria Rilke said, give up the desire for the praise of editors and critics, and go into himself, for the deep answer, to "try, as if you were one of the first men, to say what you see and experience and love and lose."

In the 1950s, while most poets were breaking out into roars of protest and whimpers of lavish confession, Creeley wrote simple, short poems that planted themselves in the memory, such as his justly famous "I Know a Man" (at left).

As I sd to my
    friend, because I am
    always talking, – John, I

sd, which was not his
name, the darkness sur-
rounds us, what

can we do against
it, or else, shall we &
why not, buy a goddamn big car,

drive, he sd, for
christ's sake, look
out where yr going.

SECOND EDITOR'S NOTE: Robert Creeley's recent works include *Memory Gardens* (1986); *Windows* (1990); *Echoes* (1994); *So There: Poems 1976-1983* (1998); *Day Book of a Virtual Poet* (1999); *Life and Death* (2000); *Just in Time* (2001), and *If I Were Writing This* (2003).

"I Know a Man," from THE COLLECTED POEMS OF ROBERT CREELEY, 1945-1975 (University of California Press: 1982). Reprinted by permission of the author.

SAD ADVICE

If it isn't fun, don't do it.
You'll have to do enough that isn't.

Such is life, like they say,
no one gets away without paying

and since you don't get to keep it
anyhow, who needs it.

— Robert Creeley

From *So There, Poems 1976-83*, New Directions, 1998. Reprinted by permission of the author.

A PERSONAL NOTE: A splash of color and charm, Sandra Cisneros stood in front of the malfunctioning microphone, tapped it once or twice, and then shrugged and smiled at

Sandra Cisneros

the restless audience at the 1997 Border Voices Poetry Fair. In yet another of the mini-miracles that have marked her long career as the country's foremost Latina author, the audience smiled as one and settled down. A wave of relaxation seemed to ripple along the seats at Balboa Park's Casa del Prado Theatre, affecting even the technicians working to repair the stubborn and aging equipment. For five minutes Cisneros stood without embarrassment on the silent stage, and then her gentle and penetrating voice lifted us all into poetry.

Sandra Cisneros was born in Chicago in 1954, the third child and only daughter in a family of seven children. She studied at Loyola University of Chicago (B.A. English 1976) and the University of Iowa (M.F.A. Creative Writing 1978). Her books include a chapbook of poetry, *Bad Boys* (Mango Press 1980); and two full-length poetry books, *My Wicked Wicked Ways* (Third Woman 1987/Random House 1992), and *Loose Woman* (Alfred A. Knopf 1994).

She has also written a number of highly successful prose works, including a collection entitled *Woman Hollering Creek and Other Stories* (Random House 1991); a children's book, *Hairs/Pelitos* (Alfred A. Knopf 1994) and the novels *The House on Mango Street* (Vintage 1991), which has sold more than two million copies; and *Caramelo* (Knopf 2002).

Before she achieved fame, Cisneros worked as a teacher and counselor to high-school dropouts, and also worked as an artist-in-the-schools where she taught creative writing at every level except first grade and pre-school.

Cisneros' poetry, stories and essays have been published in newspapers and magazines ranging from *The New York Times* to *Ms.* and *The Texas Humanist*, and have been included in numerous trade anthologies and textbooks, among them *The Oxford Book of American Short Stories*; *We Are the Stories We Tell: The Best Short Stories by North American Women Since 1945*; and *American Voices: Best Short Fiction by Contemporary Authors*.

She has received numerous awards and honors, including the MacArthur Foundation Fellowship (1995); an honorary Doctor of Humane Letters from Loyola University, Chicago (2002); the Before Columbus American Book Award (1985); the PEN Center West Award for Best Fiction of 1991 for *Woman Hollering Creek*, and many others.

ARTURITO THE AMAZING BABY OLMEC
WHO IS MINE BY WAY OF WATER

Arturito, when you were born
the hospital gasped when
they fished you from your fist of sleep,
a rude welcome you didn't like a bit,
and I don't blame you. The world's a mess.

You inherited the family sleepiness and overslept.
And in that sea the days were nacre.
When you arrived on Mexican time,
you were a wonder, a splendor, a plunder,
more royal than any Olmec
and as mysterious and grand.
And everyone said "*¡Ay!*"
or "Oh!" depending on their native tongue.

So, here you are, godchild,
a marvel that could compete with any ancient god
asleep beneath the Campeche corn. *A ti te tocó*
the aunt who dislikes kids and Catholics,
your godmother. Don't cry!
What do amazing godmothers do?
They give amazing gifts. Mine to you –
three wishes.

First, I wish you noble like Zapata,
because a man is one who guards
those weaker than himself.
Second, I wish you a Gandhi wisdom,
he knew power is not the fist,
he knew the power of the powerless.
Third, I wish you Mother Teresa generous.
Because the way of wealth is giving
yourself away to others.

Zapata, Gandhi, Mother Teresa.
Great plans! Grand joy! Amazingness!
For you, my godchild, nothing less.
These are my wishes, Arturo Olmec,
Arturito amazing boy.

— Sandra Cisneros

EDITOR'S NOTE: As with the Robert Creeley biography earlier in this book, the following was originally written for a Border Voices TV show. Again, we urge young readers (as well as curious older folks) to compare the colloquial style of this brief look at Waldman with the more traditional biographies of Adrienne Rich and Sandra Cisneros on adjoining pages. If, as you read the two approaches, you find unbidden images floating into your mind – giant salamis and wheels of cheese in a glass case, for example – this is a GOOD thing. If the words "verbal delicatessen" begin bobbing above the glass case, this is even better. A writer reaches deep into himself, and what he or she finds can surprise writer as well as audience: we live and disport ourselves in the verbal delicatessen that is the marvelous English language, and that language is both the tool and trigger of insight. That's why writers write, and readers read.

Here's a riddle for you: what do you get when you combine old-time fiddle-music with poetry about plane crashes, dogsleds and booze, all of it written and performed by a guy who perfected his craft while living like a hermit in the Alaskan wilderness? Think no phone, no running water, no TV – and lots of snow. Think of frozen misery, with an artistic twist.

Give up, but intrigued? Then allow me to introduce you to Ken Waldman, also known as "Alaska's fiddlin' poet." Ken spends five months a year roaming around the lower 48 states, plunking his fiddle and reading poems at events from New York to Oklahoma to North Carolina, and of course here in San Diego at the annual Border Voices Poetry Fair. Then – after living in a car and in cheap motels for longer than he cares to remember – he heads back to Alaska to warm up in the company of friends.

It gives me great pleasure to welcome Ken Waldman – who has been described as "William Carlos Williams behind a dogsled" – as he shares poetry and music with two students from San Diego's Border Voices Poetry Project.

SECOND EDITOR'S NOTE: Ken Waldman has published two collections of poetry: *Nome Poems* (West End Press, April 2000) and *To Live on this Earth* (West End Press; distributed by University of New Mexico Press, March 2002). His CD's – *A Week in Eek, Burnt Down House* and *Music Party* – mix poetry with old-time fiddle and banjo music. For more information, visit his web site at kenwaldman.com.

A HAPPIER DOCTOR
– for Julia

Yet another practice to begin. Magic
maybe, doctor as juggler, a dozen
roles cascading: mother and daughter; wife,
midwife, analyst; linguist
and listener; dancer, driver, chef;
healer and boss. Ah, the losses
you can now accept, the lives unlived:
local activist, global wanderer, Olympic
gymnast, grant-mad research guru, hermit
glassblower, book critic for The Times.
Some late afternoon in that blessed space
between patients, you'll have to place
the stethoscope to your own heart,
replay that path from happy to happier,
make the first move toward happiest.

— Ken Waldman

Student Poets

"Larry the Scary Ghost Kid" by Christian Ray Preston Rubio
Las Palmas Elementary

Sun, Moon and Stars

"The Continuum of Day & Night"
by Julie Nager / Standley Middle

Darkness Falls

In the middle where the dark
blanket falls is nothing.
The stars shine like diamonds
above you. The moon directs you
where to go. This is the night sky.
As if the blanket floats, you
watch it drop, and it seems like it
is miles away. The quilt of the morning
spills onto the dark. It feels
like silk. Above mountains it comes
while the sound of the river goes on.

Lizbeth Alvarez
Grade 5, San Pasqual Union
Poet-teacher: Paula Jones
Teacher: Pat Matson

IN MY BOOK OF WHISPERS

I hide atop
my cloud of dreams
and open my little box
of rainbows
to watch the shadows dance
away from the veils of color.
I dip my ffeet
into the starry sea
beneath me.
This memory
now resides
in my book of whispers.

Lina Sokolskaya
Grade 6, Lewis Middle
Poet-teacher: Jana Gardner
Teacher: Jamie Walsh

WRITE SMALL, WRITE BEAUTIFUL

I write about the blue moon.
I write about the green sun.
I write about the fiery fox flitting in the breeze.
I write about the crow flying through the mantle.
I write about the pretty painted pictures in the rocks.
I write about the lightning picking down our enemies.
I write about the human flashing ideas on her paper.
I write about the life of a leaf.
I write about the circle of life.

Rachel L. Garstang
Grade 4, Westwood Elementary
Poet-teacher: Jill Moses
Teacher: Andrea Barraugh

VAN GOGH'S STARRY NIGHT

The stars are walking in the night.
The people of the village are coming out of their houses
To see that God is protecting them wherever they go.
The sky is growing bigger, growing smaller, whirling,
Raining, drying. You may see a frown in the sky but
I can see a smile in its eyes. The people are
Talking to each other. Talking about how beautiful or strange
It looks. Before the sky was plain, now there is a beautiful
Sky, and these people are waiting to live, waiting
To die. The starry night will return to its home where people
Are longing to see it.

Carli Miller
Grade 5, San Diego Jewish Academy
Poet-teacher: Jill Moses
Teacher: Fran Miller

EINSTEIN

As a child, I dreamt of the world
and what was beyond.
As I got older, I said
to heck with the world.
Some said this was vain, but I
would do it again in a heartbeat.
Then I fell in love with the math
of the cosmos, with the sky
that gave me that simple general theory.
Now that I'm dead, I'm free
of bodily restraints, and I drift
through my life's work.
Before, I felt as if I had failed,
but from my drifting I have learned
that there is no such thing as failure
when one reaches for the stars.

Dan Driver
Grade 10, University City High
Poet-teacher: Celia Sigmon
Teacher: Sally Owen

THE NIGHT IS

The night is my little brother
playing, dreaming, running out in the cold air.
He is playing with the jungle people.
He is dreaming with the dingos in the fields
and running with the rhinos in the desert.
His eyes shine like water. He's as quiet
as the wind blowing through the spider's web,
his nose as pale as someone who's seen a ghost.
His long legs help him run with the wind
and follow the coyotes to the moon.
When he gets back home, he tells me
about how to communicate with the animals,
and I wish one night I could go with him.

John Villagrana
Grade 5, Jerabek Elementary
Poet-teacher: Celia Sigmon
Teacher: Phyllis Porter

"Runaway Dreams" by Kae Takemura / Mesa Verde Middle

DREAMS

Why do dreams enter my mind
when the sky is dark
and filled with stars?

Could it be that their small silky fingers
creep into my house
when I least expect it?

Are they aware when I
am most in need of a cheerful fantasy
and then transform my night
into a wonderland?

Do they know the perfect time
for a scare
or a night of frights?

Will there always be fingers of dreams
to show me
how marvelous
a night
can be?

Rachel Davis
Gade 7, Lewis Middle
Poet-teacher: Jana Gardner
Teacher: Kathryn Dominique

THE NIGHT SPIRIT

The Night Spirit
is creeping behind
every corner.
You can feel
that tense
moment,
that long
shaggy robe.
You walk
faster.
You can feel
its cold
sharp sickle
against your
neck, you can
hear the Night Spirit
hissing your name.
You look back
but there
is nothing.
And there you
finally go
down the stairs
and think to
yourself
that the
night is
always
dangerous.

Wesley Episcopo
Grade 5, Jerabek Elementary
Poet-teacher: Celia Sigmon
Teacher: Jean Chalupsky

"Dancing Spirit" by Kristina Kostenkova / Standley Middle

On a Clear Night

A beautiful fairy, with skin as smooth
as the silvery moon and a dress
as shimmery as the sun, sits
with her baby fairies, fragile as dolls
dancing about her with their tulip
dresses and rose petal aprons
waving white lanterns about them.
On this clear night
deep in the globe-green forest
the fairy queen tells me to come
watch them dance and learn their magic.

Gina Mortensen
Grade 4, Jerabek Elementary
Poet-teacher: Celia Sigmon
Teacher: Alison Knight

FAIRY OF THE NIGHT

The wind is a fairy
dancing through the cold night air.
It lands on my nose
and pinches it
to let me know the beauty is not a dream.

Autumn Davis
Grade 7, Lewis Middle
Poet-teacher: Jana Gardner
Teacher: Kathryn Dominique

"Fairy in the Darkness"
by Anna Lee / Standley Middle

EARLY NIGHT

Early night, silent
   water as still as stone
   white lotus and lilypads
      float like wine corks.
A fairy balances like a ballerina
   on dragonfly wings
      yellow, pink and white
      as Spring.

The moon peaks out
   behind the pencil-like reeds.
The pale fairy rides toward the water.
Her dress a bunched light blue
   like a cloud in a blue sky.

The fairy says, "When the sun comes up,
   I will go down to wait for the moon.
      When it comes up, so do I."

Samantha Castanien
Grade 4, Jerabek Elementary
Poet-teacher: Celia Sigmon
Teacher: Tammy McDaniel

How to Capture the Light of a Star

To capture the light of a star
do not think about capturing it.
Instead be free and give your own light.
Use the sun's power and the moon's tranquility.
Use the strength of a seedling pushing through
the hard compact soil.
Ask the ocean how it became so deep.
Ask the grass how it became so green.
Ask the doves how they got pure and simple
and most importantly ask the Earth how she became. . .

Teach a penguin to fly.
Teach a butterfly to swim.
Teach the people of our world to become one
and the eagle will give you wings.

Before you eat feed the dogs.
Before you sleep kiss a rose.
Before you become hostile remember the
beauty of the stars' light.

Don't become greedy or selfish.
Don't skip a single step on the stairs to
the star.
Don't think of capturing the light

and it will be given to you.

Katie Vaughan
Grade 6, Del Mar Heights Elementary
Poet-teacher: Jill Moses
Teacher: Kelly Johnson

FRIENDSHIP

I see a galaxy
beyond imagination,
stars that lead to a path
that only two
can follow.

Wesley Episcopo
Grade 5, Jerabek Elementary
Poet-teacher: Celia Sigmon
Teacher: Jean Chalupsky

"Celestial Star" by Brittney Yeo / Mesa Verde Middle

MOON FROG

The night is a frog
  with eyes like pearls
  that come from the moon
  glistening with brightness.
His feet are stars that let him
  jump fast as a comet.
When he croaks, darkness
  and shadows come out.
He can swim in pools of darkness
  and leap from star to star.
He tells me what darkness is.
  It is caution, life and mystery.

Nick Altieri
Grade 5, Jerabek Elementary
Poet-teacher: Celia Sigmon
Teacher: Mary Wood

"Undecided" by Valerie Gurrola / Central Elementary

THE BLUE FIRESTAR

The moon is like a blue fireball.
The brightness begins to blind me.
The sight is so icy cold to my touch.
The taste of the sadness makes tears
run down my face. I hear crying.
I can smell tears in the distance.
The flames taste like feeling
an ice cube in my mouth.
The moon is doomed into everlasting
space. She no longer glows like the sun,
but like a peaceful star instead.
The blue moon of loneliness cries
over everybody. When she cries,
her tears dance, as now they are free.
The ball cries out for help as she is
sinking into everlasting space.

Courtney Ferrick
Grade 8, San Pasqual Union
Poet-teacher: Jill Moses
Teacher: Michael de Neve

POWERFUL, MAGICAL ARROWS

Millions of unexpected gifts from the sky.
Nature's tiny druwmsticks.
Slender arrows of happiness from Heaven.
A cluster of miniture boomerangs
Retreating back to Earth.
An enormous living shower
Over a quiet city.
The fierce anger of a dimly lit sky.
Chilly spears plummeting from invisible buckets
Held by saddened clouds.
A sleepy artist
Absentmindedly practicing vertical lines.
A lost orchestra
Exploding with confusion.

Bryan Chu
Grade 5, Dingeman Elementary
Poet-teacher: Veronica Cunningham
Teacher: Leigh Morioka

POETRY PLANETS

Poetry is as bright as the moon.
It is like the runners
going around Saturn's rings.
Poetry is hot as the sun
and as funny as Jupiter.
Poetry is as slippery as Mars.
It's as blue as Pluto.
Poetry goes all the way to Uranus.
It's as loud as earth,
as romantic as Venus,
as fast as Mercury,
as dark as Neptune.
And what holds them all together
is the sun, full of words.

Taryn Boley
Grade 3, Hearst Elementary
Poet-teacher: Celia Sigmon
Teacher: Jean Feinstein

"My Universe" by Megan Lynn McKimmy
Las Palmas Elementary

Scorpion

The night is a scorpion
as old as the sky.
Its body skiddles
as rocks roll
down the hill.
It crawls into your shirts
to hide.
The scorpion stings
like a rattlesnake bites.
And when it talks
it says,
"Be careful because
deadly things
come out at night."

Kelly Conroy
Grade 5, Jerabek Elementary
Poet-teacher: Celia Sigmon
Teacher: Jean Chalupsky

"Night Sky" by Alex Scherling / Standley Middle

Owl

The moon is an owl,
as quiet as the night,
as white and silent
but full of misery.
Its white silky face
is waiting, waiting,
poking its head through
the ribbons of the trees.
The owl is full of questions.
Its red beady eyes
like rubies with devils inside,
have all the secrets of the night
like why the moon has holes.

Kimberly Maxon
Grade 4, Jerabek Elementary
Poet-teacher: Celia Sigmon
Teacher: Christina Martin

MILKY WAY COYOTE

The Milky Way is like a coyote
swift and sly as he walks
across the cloudy sky.
He is hidden among the shadows
as he creeps through my bedroom window.
He spys my cat, thinking it's dinner.
But I throw Coyote out
and back he goes to the heavens,
still looking for a midnight snack.
Before he leaves he tells me,
"The night is a beautiful thing.
Don't be afraid of it."

Emily Gould
Grade 4, Jerabek Elementary
Poet-teacher: Celia Sigmon
Teacher: Nancy Walters

"Sun Wolves" by Sandra Real / Southwest Middle

HOWLING AT THE MOON

A timber wolf,
white as a cloud
black as charcoal,
howling at the moon.
The moon, yellow
as a gold coin,
shines on the mountains
blue as the deep ocean
underneath the night sky.

Ryan Moelter
Grade 4, Jerabek Elementary
Poet-teacher: Celia Sigmon
Teacher: Kathy Comina

STAR SNAKE

The night is a star snake's diamond eyes.
Its black silvery scales like the moon
shining in the darkness.
Its rounded nose poking at the pillows
like they were white rats
glimmering in the star's bright light.
It slithers like a dark shadow
hiding from the light.
It flies overhead, ready to strike.
Then it says to me, "Don't be afraid.
I'm here for you."

Markus Raimondi
Grade 5, Jerabek Elementary
Poet-teacher: Celia Sigmon
Teacher: Kathie Lloyd

"Shooting Gleaming Star"
by Anthony Corona / Las Palmas Elementary

SHADOW SNAKE

The night is like a shadow snake
black as a crow's feather
with eyes as white as an untanned man.
He feeds on one thing and one thing only…
my socks.
He slithers up the wall and peers at me
from the ceiling. He cuts off the heads
of my stuffed animals with his tail.
Call me crazy, but there he is, staring at me
with a stuffed animal head on his tail.
With glaring eyes he says,
"WASH YOUR SOCKS."

Shane Sprague
Grade 5, Jerabek Elementary
Poet-teacher: Celia Sigmon
Teacher: Mary Wood

Sky On Fire

Shadowy birds, dark and mysterious
like the night sky, bare trees
growing from an orange juice lake.
I hear the shadows, the egrets
splashing through the silky water.
The sky is on fire,
the mountains dark as coal.
This is what it would be like
if it were day and night together.

John Moon
Grade 4, Jerabek Elementary
Poet-teacher: Celia Sigmon
Teacher: Tammy McDaniel

"Night & Day" by Moira Ogata / Standley Middle

WHEN I WAKE UP

When I wake up in the morning
it feels like my eyes are on fire.

My body feels broken into pieces
like a dropped mirror.

I feel crunchy, like a piece of toast
and slow and tired like a creeping snail.

Abdisalam Mumin
Grade 5, Marshall Elementary
Poet-teacher: Johnnierenee Nelson
Teacher: John Bartholomew

THE BLACK CAT

The night is like a black cat,
its eyes bright as stars.
Its body is dark as midnight,
   camoflauged in the alley,
   hiding in the trash can,
   invisible in the night.
It is saying,
"The night is magical."

Curtis Arnold
Grade 4, Jerabek Elementary
Poet-teacher: Celia Sigmon
Teacher: Nancy Walters

"City Night" by Angeline Salvani / Morse High

MELTING INTO THE LIGHT OF DAY

Panthera Tigris Tigris,
the tiger
a silent shadow embodied in the long grass
staying low, quiet as a feather aloft
falling from the sky, fluttering past
intense orange color in a realm of green and gold
melting into the light of day
as your lethal claws unfold
stalking, watching, eyeing your prey
now within a few strides
CHARGE!
startling the deer, ready to flee this place
never witnessing a danger so large
caught in a deadly embrace
the bright flaming tiger
elegant among peaceful scenery
violent, full of immense power
an orange amber eyed fury
swift as a dream
you strike like lightening
seen but unheard
Panthera Tigris Tigris,
the tiger
the silent stalker, unnoticed, endangered...

Jessa Balcita
Grade 9, Morse High
Poet-teacher: Glory Foster
Teacher: Carol Zupkas

"Sunrise" by Hieu Phan / Morse High

THE RED SUNSET

A red sunset
Beating on the ocean shore
A fire shadow on a rock
Two tarantulas making their webs
Tomatoes on a vine
The stripes on the American flag
Lava erupting out of a volcano
The heart
The blood of the revolutionary war

Brandon Poss
Grade 3, Jerabek Elementary
Poet-teacher: Roxanne Kilbourne
Teacher: Sonia Longfellow

Sunset Chicken

Inside my heart
is a blazing plate of orange chicken
bright as a sunset
with fifteen amber egg rolls
sprinkled with gold.

Inside my heart
is shaved ice
cold as the North Pole
with jade, jet, crimson rust
robin egg and copper colors
like the Northern Lights.

David Nuñez
Grade 4, Central Elementary
Poet-teacher: Johnnierenee Nelson
Teacher: Christine Calabria

NATURE'S TURN

SPRING

Ribbons of cloud
      are a stairway to the sun.
         Winter's trees
       drawn in spiraling black ink
climb in awe.

Samantha C. Peterson
Grade 8, Lewis Middle
Poet-teacher: Jana Gardner
Teacher: Kathryn Dominique

DESERT SPRING

Through the car window I see
    wind blowing the bright green cottonwoods
    tiny pink flowers blooming on the sand
    kids riding their bicycles
    while cars pass on the hot asphalt
    jack-rabbits hopping from bush to bush
    reptiles coming out of hibernation.
This time of year there is no snow or rain
falling from the sky.
But I will always remember the way
I wait for summer to pass,
playing in the hot streets
below Table Top Mountain
while ocotillos bloom in the tall hills.

Carina Zavala
Grade 4, Jacumba Elementary
Poet-teacher: Celia Sigmon
Teacher: Susan Barry

"From Out of the Ashes"
by Arjie-Abegail Lopez / Morse High

The End and the Beginning

I'm all the green of the world
the grass, leaves, trees and bushes
I'm the winter: cold, white and brutal
the whispers of everyone in this world
silent and full of mystery
I'm a circle: rolling to my destinations in mere seconds
I'm a pool of water
inviting all those who wish to refresh and play
I'm a Saturday welcoming the end and the beginning
I'm the minerals of the earth, precious
providing ideas to the ones finding me
the gems of the earth: creating happiness and bestowing
beauty
The sunset and sunrise
telling about the end and the beginning
The clock: measuring events and major happenings
the light and darkness: fears and hope
I'm a burrito: satisfying one's hunger
The stars: guiding those who are lost
A dog: loyal to friends and family
An ocean: vast and full of secrets
The universe: a place never explored thoroughly
I am me: a special and unique person

David Arellano, Jr.
Grade 7, Southwest Middle
Poet-teacher: Glory Foster
Teacher: Pat Koob

UNCHANGED

I am the earth.
  I hide in the past
    turning creatures to stone.
My red clay builds walls.
  My pale stones pave roads.
I am shaped by water
  charred by fire
    moved by wind.
But I stand eternal
  to house the living
    and bury the dead.

Daniel Zengel
Grade 10. University City High
Poet-teacher: Celia Sigmon
Teacher: Sally Owen

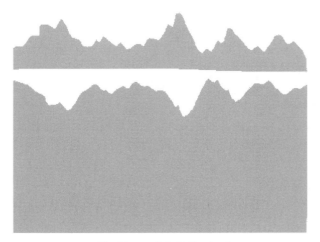

"The Mountain's Reflection"
by David MacAdam / Standley Middle

LISTEN TO IRIS

after a painting by Rafal Olbinski

Iris,
the beloved princess.
Her voice
soft,
sweet,
gentle
as the wind,
beautiful as the harp.
If she were here today,
she would sing for us.
But she is no longer here.
Sometimes
on a calm gentle breeze
you can hear her voice
beautiful as ever
drifting in a deep valley
to where the iris would grow.

Vanessa Vincent
Grade 5, St.Patrick's School
Poet-teacher: Jill Moses
Teacher: Karen Hoyle

Nature

Trees play together while the wind flies swiftly past
Stars shine brightly in the darkest night
Flowers talk as soft as the wind
The grass dances while everything else is still
The rain beats on a house in the middle of nowhere
Vines walk slowly around a huge tree
Everything is alive.

Katie Stewart
Grade 4, St. Patrick's School
Poet-teacher: Jill Moses
Teacher: Joan DeCottes

"Garden of Peace" by Bernadette P. Magno / Morse High

YO SOY IMAGINACIÓN

Yo soy el sol brillando al amanecer
Yo soy la lluvia callendo sin cesar
Yo soy una hoja suicidandose en el Otoño
Yo soy un pájaro cantando sin parar
Yo soy una flor
Trayendo felicidad
Yo soy la emoción,
Que llena tu vida de alegría
Yo soy las palabras que salen de tu boca
Yo soy un color que brilla en tu vida
Yosoy un reloj
Contando los minutos de tu vida
Yo soy un calendario
Contando los días de mi vida
Yo soy la imaginación de los niños
En otro mundo diferente
Yo soy una llave
Para abrir tu corazón
Yo soy un pie para dar un paso más a la vida
Yo soy yo, y nadie me puede cambiar

"Coronado" by Brian Bacsal / Morse High

I am Imagination

I am the sun shining during sunrise.
I am the rain falling endlessly.
I am a leaf that suicides during fall
I am a bird singing without stopping.
I am a flower
bringing happiness.
I am the emotion
that fills your life with joy.
I am the words that come out of your mouth.
I am a color that shines in your life.
I am a clock
counting the minutes of your life.
I am a calendar
counting the days of my life.
I am the imagination of children
in another, different world.
I am a key
for opening your heart.
I am a foot that takes a step forward in life.
I am me, and nobody can change me.

Translated by Francisco Bustos

Stephanie Gurrola
Grade 6, Kimball Elementary
Poet-teacher: Francisco Bustos
Teacher: Beneranda J. Calderón

Yo Soy la Flor de Jazmin

Yo soy la flor de jazmín
que se abre en la mañana
para ver la luz del sol.
También soy el girasol
que abre sus pestañas
y al girar, refleja su luz en la ventana.
Soy un poeta que escribe su sentimiento
y lo que lleva dentro.

Yo soy la hija del Dios todo poderoso
que me cuida y me cubre
con su manto precioso.
Soy como un esclavo que queda en libertad.
Soy alguien que da un paso
para no volver atrás.
Así soy yo porque así me hizo Dios.

I AM THE JASMINE FLOWER

I am the jasmine flower
That opens in the morning
To see the sun's light.
I am also the sunflower
That opens its eyebrows
Reflecting its light on a window as it turns.
I am a poet that writes her feelings
And what she has within.

I am the daughter of God almighty
Who takes care of me and covers me
With a precious mantle.
I am like a freed slave.
I am someone who takes a step
Forward not to turn back.
That is how I am, because God made me so.

Dora Alicia Álvarez Juárez
Grade 8, Casa-Hogar Lirio de los Valles Tijuana
Poet-teacher: Francisco Bustos
Director: Sara Duña

How to Dance with a Leaf

1. Climb up a tall oak tree.
2. Find a branch that has leaves
dressed in their prettiest colors.
*Tip – the ones with red dresses
are usually the best dancers.
3. Ask the leaf politely if it would like to dance.
4. If it says yes,
jump up and down with excitement.
(They will dance best if they know
you are excited to dance with them.)
5. Grab the leaf's hand and start to sway back and forth.
6. Soon the leaf will lead the dance
down all the way to the ground.
7. Enjoy the spins and dips;
just remember to hold the leaf tight.

Michelle Peltz
Grade 10, Heritage Christian
Poet-teacher: Jill Moses
Teacher: Cathy Peltz

"Forestry" by Aline Xayasouk / Morse High

ODE TO THE TREE

Old but strong
Green as grass
Brown as bricks
Flowing like a river
The trunk breaks into branches
The branches break into twigs
Just like a lake flows into rivers
And a river flows into a stream
And a stream flows into the flower and fruit
Of a tree.

Oh tree, why are you so mysterious?
Where is your soul,
Where is your blood,
And what do you feel?

Rafael Cosman
Grade 5, San Diego Jewish Academy
Poet-teacher: Jill Moses
Teacher: Fran Miller

My Rock and Your Rock

Your rock may be solid, but mine is hollow
and nothing can change that.
Your rock may be drab and gray,
but mine is sparkling with the light of stars at night
and deep with the depth of an ocean.
Your rock may be plain like a square,
but mine is like an ear listening and recording the past
or a hammer digging deep in history
or possibly a beak of a bird helping keep us alive.
Your rock may be new and jagged,
but mine is a piece of history
that survives wind and rain.
Your rock may be useless, but mine is useful
as a compass
when you're lost.

William Creed
Grade 4, Westwood Elementary
Poet-teacher: Jill Moses
Teacher: Andrea Barraugh

Summer Sun on a Rock

It is a rock blanketed by summer sun.
It is a snail's adagio, showing off a silver trail.
You see it in the puddle that the willow dips into.
Your eyes draw it from a lily freckled with dew.
It is your silk jacket you just purchased for your party.
You love its soft music.
You seek it in an old flower,
withered with the passage of time.
It is serenity.

Caitlin Hicks
Grade 4, Ada Harris Elementary
Poet-teacher: Jill Moses
Teacher: Susan Roughen

"Mystical Mushroom" by Pamela Maza / Southwest Middle

"Cloudy, Cloudy Life" by Lauren Miller / Standley Middle

THE HIGH SIERRAS

Green is the High Sierras reaching to the sky
Leaves on the pine tree
clinging onto the trunk
The wind roaring
A freshly picked Granny Smith apple
The long thick grass on the prairie
where coyotes wait to pounce on their prey
The ocean at sunset
whispering to the shore
The smell of the dark woods
The sound of frogs
in the murky swamp
The weed in the desert
falling to its side

Ryan Merrill
Grade 3, Jerabek Elementary
Poet-teacher: Roxanne Kilbourne
Teacher: Sonia Longfellow

PINE CONE MYSTERY

Oh, Pine Cone
You are the mystery of the world
With layers of eyes
Encircling your exterior
Eyes that see all
As you spin and spin
Around the universe
Your layers are like the shapes
In a kaleidoscope
Or the rings on a turtle's shell
Concealing what is hidden
But as the years go by
You explode like a grenade
Releasing your essence
Oh, Pine Cone
Your essence is the realm of the galaxy
The essence of knowledge
That man has tried so hard to achieve
But why?
Why do you lay lifeless on the ground?
Are you not that celestial being?
Oh, Pine Cone
You are truly the mystery of the world.

Daryl Fulgencio
Grade 10, Morse High
Poet-teacher: Glory Foster
Teacher: Cynthia Larkin

SLEEP IN A DRAWER

inspired by "Mesa de noche" by Mario Rangel

It is night
Sleep has come
White flowers grow furiously
The sweet smell floats all around
One by one
Little blossoms poke their heads
Through the jungle ocean of jade green leaves
Venturing out to the world of night
"You are overflowing, my dear flower"
Tints of green blotched on the skin
A young yellow lemon says
"I don't care"
Replies from the constantly growing flowers
echo in my ears
"The human is asleep
They can't intrude in our world now
It is our time to grow"
One after the other blossoms reveal their eyes
To the outside world
Pastel pink, yellow, and purple peek out
From the white hidden inside
Their carefully wrapped petals
A precious present
More delicate than glass
I sleep down below
Under the continuously growing flowers
Under the arguing adolescent lemon
In the small drawer
Of the table you sit upon
In your black overflowing vase

Don't bother me
Sleep has come over to my house
I will awake
When sleep has gone
I will not bother
Your growth or argument
So let me be
In the world of dreams
In my own comfortable bed
In the drawer of a table
In front of the baby blue wall
In the safety of the amber smell
Away from reality
Darkness has come
Sleep is in my house
Please leave me alone
To my own soft world
Of sleep

Mai Yamaguchi
Grade 8, Stanley Middle
Poet-teacher: Glory Foster
Teacher: Reissa Schrager-Cole

"Belle Rose" by Anastasia Volnova / Standley Middle

Autumn

Through the windows
a breeze rustles the soft branches
children laugh and crunch the leaves
birds waltz through the trees
and the sweet aroma of pumpkin
fills the air
Autumn awakening...

Anna Godinho
Grade 7, Mesa Verde Middle
Poet-teacher: Glory Foster
Teacher: Joie Nolasco

"Happy Days" by Carl V. Pasquale
Standley Middle

THE FALL WILDERNESS

The cormorants hang on trees
like the fruits of summer.
In the motionless breeze of Fall
trees turn black as the night sky
in front of the setting sun, and the river
is smooth as the orange sky.
Black mountains stop the river
from flooding the wilderness.
The sky glows as if
there were a fire in the distance.
The river says, "Stop and relax.
Enjoy life while you can."

Rachel Rios
Grade 5, Jerabek Elementary
Poet-teacher: Celia Sigmon
Teacher: Phyllis Porter

WINDS OF CHANGE

inspired by Jose Clemente Orozco

In the winter night I find men before me
Men with ordinary lives, fighting the coldness of the wind
And yet something's amiss...

They dwell upon unclear paths
Thinking of things to say and the things better left unsaid
They walk in circles, contemplating
In the darkness, in the fallout, in the biting wind
Like the similar hats they wear, they wear the same burden
 of searching for something...
They wander and wonder, looking for movement
Looking for something to stumble and fumble on...

Blue and slow each step takes a century in my time
But look!
A storm approaches, a sign of revolution
A breeze passes by, a sign of redemption
A golden ray descends from heaven, a sign of a new age
Breaking the era of idleness and silent chaos
 that has befallen these men

In the winter night, I find that this season will come and go
As with the other seasons of history
These men will find themselves in the bloom
 of new beginnings
And will lose themselves in the treacherous blizzard
The winter night is an age of confusion, dark and cold
Followed by revolution, redemption and a new age...
Till the cycle begins again...

Mikael Cabal
Grade 9, Morse High
Poet-teacher: Glory Foster
Teacher: Carol Zupkas

"Anthropomorphism"
by Andrew Largoza / Morse High

74

SORRY

after art by Magritte

A man is dressed in deep black, full of sorrow,
hiding his burnt sorry face behind an apple.
Black is eating the green apple
taking over the man's feelings.
The dark clouds block out the sun.
I feel the man's hand, boney
but soft and pale. His tie red with love.
Someone has died. I hear him
mumbling something about family.
I smell fresh wind blowing.
I taste the apple – tart, not sweet,
sour as the taste of death.

Oliver Weber
Grade 4, Jerabek Elementary
Poet-teacher: Celia Sigmon
Teacher: Angela Tucker

SHIMMERING JEWELS

Something about blue
Is like tulips
Shimmering in the meadow,
Butterflies flying,
Twinkling in the early morning,
The smell of the ocean
Full of white sea salt,
An airplane soaring
With a roaring engine
Rumbling in the blue sky.

Kaylyn Harris
Grade 3, Jerabek Elementary
Poet-teacher: Roxanne Kilbourne
Teacher: Sonia Longfellow

Ever Radiant

I am the radiant albino tiger.
Watch me as I jump swiftly from tree to tree.
I taste the blood of an unsuspecting spider monkey
That was aimlessly swinging about.
I feel the coarse bark on the bottom of my callused paws.
I smell the smoke of the hunters and I hear their shouts.
They are searching for me; they want my fur.
Again, I will leave my home
To travel deeper into the rainforest.
How long until the sweet smell of the trees
Or the sound of the gurgling brook
Will no longer be there?
The rain forest will die and I will die with it.
No place to run, no place to hide,
Just smoke, and ash, and fire, and death.

Alyx Barbeau
Grade 7, Heritage Christian
Poet-teacher: Jill Moses
Teacher: Patricia Barbeau

Striped Tigers

Striped tigers
inside my fuzzy heart

zoom past the sandy beach
and the slimy seaweed in my world

roar with the wavy, electric ocean
of my imagination.

Charlene Stoudenmire
Grade 3, Central Elementary
Poet-teacher: Johnnierenee Nelson
Teacher: Delia Robinson

"Cat Eyes" by Kysa Tran / Mesa Verde Middle

Centennial Polar Bear

White fur
snowy white fur.
This is a polar bear
with beetle black eyes
staring at the snow
as white as himself.
In the circle of life
hibernation slows down
everything. Maybe you
should try it
this winter.

Jeramiah Andries
Grade 3, Jacumba Elementary
Poet-teacher: Celia Sigmon
Teacher: Susan Barry

"Snuggly Panda" by Ashley Peterson / Mesa Verde Middle

DIAMOND SNAKE

I am a glacier
a rushing, gushing river
in slow mo
Don't tell me to hurry up
I'm going as fast as I can
cutting deep into the earth
I travel from mountain peaks to valleys
like a roller coaster snail
and when the ride is over
I melt away
But wait don't go
The ride will start again soon
and you can see me
like a snake made of diamonds

Julian Gold
Grade 8, Stanley Middle
Poet-teacher: Glory Foster
Teacher: Reissa Schrager-Cole

ODE TO THE AMETHYST

Oh, amethyst
You are a sunken treasure
buried deep within the depths
of the murky ocean.
You are the stars scattered
across the bright sky, eternally glistening.
You are the tall pyramid in the desert
standing still and stable
in the unbearable heat.

Oh, amethyst
You are the fireworks
shining above the night sky.
You are the flower bed of roses
with dew shimmering brightly
off your radiant colored petals.

Oh, amethyst
You are the ocean glittering
brightly under the moonlight.
You are the celestial star in the spotlight
illuminating the sandy beach with speckles of light.

Kayla Cordova
Grade 7, Mesa Verde Middle
Poet-teacher: Glory Foster
Teacher: Daniel Fleming

OH, THE SADNESS I FEEL

When I'm at
the animal shelter,
the sadness builds up inside me
like a log house being built
from top to bottom.
I hear all the animals cry
as I do
in my heart.
I see the wetness
under their eyes
as I hold them in my arms.
I feel their soft skin.
It kills me to see them
in their cages with no family
to care for them or play with them.
Oh, the sadness I feel.

Allison Arebalo
Grade 5, San Pasqual Union
Poet-teacher: Paula Jones
Teachers: Wendy Snapp and Karalee Gorham

"Underwater World" by Andrew Cheu / Mesa Verde Middle

"Freedom" by Celia Ma / Mesa Verde Middle

THE CHILD RIDER

The child balances
On his ruby horse
In the blue circus tent
Of willow branches
And memories
Standing upright
With his bouquet
Of wildflowers
His frightened soul
Is comforted
By an ivory-white
Dove

Emma Townsend-Merino
Grade 8, Lewis Middle
Poet-teacher: Jana Gardner
Teacher: Kathryn Dominique

ODE TO RANGER

He's brown
as toffee
with patches
of snowflakes
thrown in.
A handsome dog,
his eyes sparkle
with mischievousness.
No doubt
he has chewed
my pencil.
His ears hang down
floppy as wet paper.
They go up when
he's excited.
He laps up water.
It sounds like waves crashing.
He barks,
a playful bark,
like the shriek of a young child
on a swing.
His tail stands up.
His ears are good
as radio detectors
four times as good as ours.
When he stands next to me,
I feel protected
like a young child
snuggled in her mother's arms.

Susanna Fenstermacher
Grade 6, Del Mar Heights Elementary
Poet-teacher: Jill Moses
Teacher: Keri Gibson

I See a Mouse

Every night there's a mouse
on my window sill.
He walks with tiny claws
and two arms as furry as a cat.
He wears glasses
as small as a flea,
and he's always thinking
about algebra equations.
He's as gray as a wolf
but not that fat, his smile
as big as a person's fist,
his teeth as white as paper.
He's as smart as Albert Einstein.

Deryl Lam
Grade 5, Jerabek Elementary
Poet-teacher: Celia Sigmon
Teacher: Phyllis Porter

"The Crazy Cat"
by Miriam Villanueva / Las Palmas Elementary

COOL CAT

I hear jazz music in the lounge,
hanging out with all my feline friends.
"The performer tonight is the famous
Smokey & Friends," meowed the announcer
as he spotlighted each black cat,
who all played in B flat.
But one had on her chest a white star
and she played a bass guitar.
Smokey blew his sax and sang,
"Music is our life. Let it set you free."

Shelbie Schauf
Grade 5, Jerabek Elementary
Poet-teacher: Celia Sigmon
Teacher: Mary Wood

MY CAT

My Cat, how do you use your tail?
Dear One, I use my tail to keep my balance.
My Cat, how do you use your sharp claws?
Dear One, I use my sharp claws to climb.
My Cat, how do you use your pointy teeth?
Dear One, I use my pointy teeth to eat food.
My Cat, why can't you make tears?
Dear One, so I don't cry when you go.

Merissa Washalaski
Grade 3, Spreckles Elementary
Poet-teacher: Gabriela Anaya Valdepeña
Teacher: Lane Campbell

ODE TO A WAVE

A wave,
when it breaks
you can see
beautiful white horses.
You can hear
its heart beating
fast, against the beach.
It is as huge as
a dinosaur and
as small as a mouse.
You can feel the
water spray into
your face as it breaks
like fighting fists,
wave and beach.
When calm it
sings so beautifully.
When you surf it
you feel like you're
in a green curler.
You feel cold and
warm at the very
same time.

Kyla Peterson
Grade 5, St. Patrick's School
Poet-teacher: Jill Moses
Teacher: Karen Hoyle

ODE TO THE WATERS

To the waters that give me life
To the waters that are re-born in every animal
To the free living waters that flow through me,
      through earth and sun
To the waters that mouth the song of the sky and
      form life from death
To the waters that give health to earth and mammal
To the blue silver waters of the waterfall that echo
      through the earth worm
To the waters that give and take life.

Sammy Köhler Ahmed
Grade 3, Spreckles Elementary
Poet-teacher: Gabriela Anaya Valdepeña
Teacher: Lane Campbell

"Geronimo" by Nancy Oudommahavanh / Morse High

OCEAN

Sometimes
like a piece of
glass constantly
shifting in its
sleep.

Tori Gudmundson
Grade 5, San Pasqual Union
Poet-teacher: Paula Jones
Teacher: Pat Matson

"Life Filled with Restrictions"
by Colleen Bordon / Morse High

FISHING

The *whoosh* of the pole being cast.
The steady *rrrr* of the motor.
The *bang* of the tackle box closing.
The *plop* of the lure hitting the water.
The exciting *zzzz* of the fish jumping.
The upsetting *snap* of the line breaking.
The *grrr* of the angler getting mad.
The *pop* of the boat docking.
The *boom* of the car door closing.
The *vroom* of the car speeding off.

Wesley Zimmerman
Grade 7, Greenfield Middle
Poet-teacher: Georgette James
Teacher: Allison Wittman

Swim

Strong, strong,
I am strong
in the water
surrounded by warmth
like a mother's womb.
I am safe
and strong
watching silver bubbles
illuminated by golden light
soar by.
Sometimes
they cling to my hands
like living things,
then fly up to join
the silvery surface
where my golden hand
is reflected.
It arcs up
through cold black air
and gracefully
dives back into bliss.
I am no longer in the water,
I am the water.

Kathryn Mogk
Grade 6, Lewis Middle School
Poet-teacher: Jana Gardner
Teacher: Jamie Walsh

Salton Sea

The dark birds land on trees
as soon as the sky turns orange.
The dark trees have no leaves
but the birds have the water.
When the sky turns blue
they'll roost in the mountains
and when the sun sinks down
they will fly to the trees
to fish and take their dinner.
As the sad sky falls
the lake will be deserted.

Sebastien Razavi
Grade 3, Hearst Elementary
Poet-teacher: Celia Sigmon
Teacher: Jean Feinstein

Pool Reflections

Sweet and quiet,
reflections on the water lilies
swimming all around with nobody there.
Just softness—
no words, no whispers,
not a sound.
Only a pool with reflections,
and lilies.

Monica Minor
Grade 5, Marshall Elementary
Poet-teacher: Jana Gardner
Teacher: Leslie Johnson

OCEAN

It roars and it growls.
It's full of clicks, groans and whistles.
You hear it through the deck,
You smell the salt and brine.
It slaps the beach
Then flows back on itself.
With a slap and a hiss
It never stops moving.
Standing on the beach all I hear is
Roar, whoosh, slap and hiss
Over and over again.

Hollis Liebe
Grade 7, Greenfield Middle
Poet-teacher: Georgette James
Teacher: Allison Wittman

"See Under the Sea" by Naomi Tamashiro / Morse Hish

THE ROAR OF THAILAND

The roar of the waves
The whisper of the palm tree
The tiptoe of the crab
Speaks to me
The pearl of shells
The shimmer of the sand
Speaks to me
The honking of the cars
The earthquake of trucks
Speaks to me
The strong wind of the subway
Speaks to me
And my heart is filled with joy

Esther Klijn
Grade 3, Jerabek Elementary
Poet-teacher: Roxanne Kilbourne
Teacher: Sonia Longfellow

"Little Lost Island of Paradise"
by Natasha Makarova / Standley Middle

WHEN DID IT START?

When did the world begin?
Did someone wave their hand across space
and as a magician would
make the world appear?
Or did it originate from smaller organisms
over time evolving?
Maybe some god got bored,
flicked a switch and said,
"Let there be light."
And there we were,
patiently waiting like caterpillars in a chrysalis.
Maybe God spins us on his finger
like his basketball
or like spinning thread.
Maybe we are just one thought in a whirlpool of
thoughts. A little boy thinks us up
with each passing minute,
giggling each time a peacock's tail flares,
crying when someone in Greenland is hit,
in awe when another Neil Armstrong is born,
bored by our everyday problems, having seen them
at least a million times.

Jaclyn Sieloff-Woodson
Grade 6, Farb Middle
Poet-teacher: Paula Jones
Teacher: Donna Rankin

Rites of Passage

"Complete the Puzzle" by John James Valenteros / Morse High

The 4-F Drop

A raindrop falls from the sky,
dodges the trees and glides
through the air. Then it is
        going
        going
SPLAT! gone.
It hits the ground and it is
        dead!
        dead!
        dead!
"Man down," says the cloud.

Max Schweiger
Grade 5, Jerabek Elementary
Poet-teacher: Celia Sigmon
Teacher: Kathie Lloyd

JUST BLACK

Black is an awesome color,
a color to build off of.
Black leaves room for thought,
not loud, but mysterious, scary
unknown and blank.
Black is the dark sky at night.
Black is off: computer screens
television, thoughts all blank.
Black is winter at midnight
laying face up on your bed
seeing nothing, or maybe something.
Black is not knowing what is next.
Black is nothing, yet everything.

Chris Gallagher
Grade 5, Jerabek Elementary
Poet-teacher: Celia Sigmon
Teacher: Kathie Lloyd

THROUGH THE EYES

I am
A loud whispering
Noise making
Peace making, war starting
Non driving teenage girl

Through the eyes of my family
I am
A crashing thunderbolt
Released from oblivion
A cheesecake loving, mango eating, peanut butter
        Girl Scout cookie enjoyer
A rainbow of joyful yellow life
Full of red love
Selfish green
Blue difficulty
And gentle consideration
Appearing as a circle leaping blob
        Around the house halls
Passing like whistling wind in the night
In the eyes of my friends
I appear as the other side of the moon
Shooting out spontaneous predictability

At times
Raging sadness
Followed by a scissor-like mind
Basketball shooting, music listening
    Teenage friend
Unique
But as "everyday" as the stars
In the never-ending soul of space
As happy as Friday's joy...

Elissa L. Hill
Grade 10, Morse High
Poet-teacher: Glory Foster
Teacher: Cynthia Larkin

"The Sounds" by Andrew Largoza / Morse High

MORE THAN AN OSTRICH FEATHER

The ostrich feather is like a broom
sweeping away
all the memories of the past.
It is like a pen writing
the future for everyone.
It is like a toy tickling your neck
when you relax on the lonely grass.
It is like a fan
blowing away the bad things in life
and breathing in all the good.
It is like a palm tree
swaying back and forth
as the wind blows
on the lonely island.
It is like the big bright moon
shining over the dark city
at night.

Alessandra Alarcon
Grade 7, Southwest Middle
Poet-teacher: Glory Foster
Teacher: Pat Koob

"A Walk in the Park" by Krist Nostrates / Las Palmas Elementary

Default

I am just another person, just another story
too small to matter, too big to ignore.
My childhood smells like sawdust and the ocean
like nothing and everything all at once.
The rain tastes like the answer to a question
everyone is too afraid to ask.
The mirror reflects what I wish wasn't there
and hides what I should be proud of.
I come from the land of overly-optimistic cynics
of lost causes and bad jokes.
The door home has no handle, no knocker.
Perhaps that's why it leads to Amsterdam.

I am the king, all beauty and strength.
My childhood smells like maidens and feasts.
The rain tastes like a fine 1921 Chardonnay.
In the mirror I see perfect black hair and tanned skin,
that slightly foreign mysterious look.
I come from vacation and am going on holiday.
When I come to the door, it opens gently
for I have the key that fits it all
and all that leads to arrogance.

When I look in the mirror, I see
all that could possibly be expected:
a middle-aged pseudo-trendy businessman
a six foot tall Caucasian male in a cheap suit
with a childhood that smells home-cooked.
I came from suburbia and I'm going there now.
The door, I see, is already open.
It leads to a cubicle in an architecturally boring office,
to boredom, to monotony, to happily-ever-after.

Riley Guza
Grade 10, University City High
Poet-teacher: Celia Sigmon
Teacher: Sally Owen

"Individuality" by Marian Daniells / Mesa Verde Middle

SELF-CONFIDENCE

I am the feeling you get when you know
    You have the ability to act.

If I were music I would be a piano concerto.

If I were a bird I would be the magnificent eagle
    That soars through the Canadian sky.

If I were a taste I would be Crème Brulée.

If I were something you could touch
I would be the smoothest stone in the sea.

    I am self-confidence.

Steven Walker
Grade 7, Greenfield Middle
Poet-teacher: Georgette James
Teacher: Emily Sabin

Downtown Puberty

I am not an indestructible tower
In the center of a crowded street
I am not a tulip growing in a garden
Of infallible pigments
I am not time
Organized, continuous, and punctual
I am not a toy box popping out
Perfect in measure and color
I am stronger than a glass
Not easily broken
I am a blade of grass
One, equal among many
I am the seasons
Only four but changing with grace
I am a junk drawer
Container of many different things
Forgotten and remembered
But precious like unknown antiques.

Jenevive Mendoza
Grade 10, Morse High
Poet-teacher: Glory Foster
Teacher: Cynthia Larkin

Filling Your Shoes

Living on the edge
Eating pie with Don McClean
My life is perpetually stuck
In this rock and roll dream.

Freewheeling, free falling
You ain't got nothing, honey, if it ain't free.
Come on, baby, set the night on fire
For the rest of eternity.

These monuments that peer into my soul
Just give me the blues.
Their dark shadows make me realize
I can never fill your shoes.

I followed the tambourine man
Down the Yellow Brick Road.
Said hello to Dolly, had a laugh with Leroy Brown
But nowhere was new to be found.

As hell's bells came crashing
Through a purple haze sky
My heart was painted black
As I watched sweet emotion die.

Took a room at Hotel California
To try and find my peace, but found only Ziggy Stardust
Who said "Hey, mate, let it be"
And my pain was finally released.

In that instant, it came clear.
Though I'll never fill the shoes of mighty men like these,
I'll do the only thing I know:
Just keep on being me.

Zack Warma
Grade 10, University City High
Poet-teacher: Celia Sigmon
Teacher: Sally Owen

"Rockin' the Galaxy" by Daniel Leach / Morse High

Regret Keeps Falling

Regret is like an apple
Like an eye, it sometime sees
Only what it wants to see
It is like a snowflake that keeps falling
The feeling is so plastic and surreal
Regret tastes sour
But goes on and on
Like the circle of a doughnut
You can't get rid of the sunburn of regret
Nor the waxy feeling covering the truth
Like a shooting star, you can't go back
Regret sounds solid like a bowling ball
Hitting the pins getting louder and louder
Until you hear the drum roll climax
And see that regret is a hollow Christmas ornament

Lauren Reyes
Grade 10, Morse High
Poet-teacher: Glory Foster
Teacher: Carol Zupkas

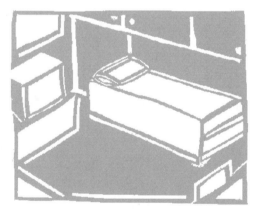

"Sanctuary" by Christian Adviento / Morse High

THE TOUGH JOURNEY OF LIFE

My life
is a long journey.
Filled with road signs
stoplights and traffic.
Slow down
Speed up
Stop!

My life
is filled with road bumps.
Crossroads confront me.
A devilish python's glare
tries to hypnotize me.
But an inner strength
makes me look away.

My life
is filled with tough choices.
My imagination and creativity
get stuck in traffic.
My knowledge
flies by at breakneck speed.
My personality
cruises at a steady speed.

I tremble
with every decision I make.
My life
is a long journey...

Andrew Occiano
Grade 7, Mesa Verde Middle
Poet-teacher: Glory Foster
Teacher: Marycay Densmore

In That Moment

Open the door
Jump on in
Turn to the wall
Shake hands with Spielberg
He's off to finish his film
Jump back and fall to the floor
Just in time as T-Rex
returns to its place in time
Taste antiseptic air
Steely interior of a death star
Reel and Wheel, red clashes with blue
Darth Vader verses Luke
The crowd explodes
Commotion in the top left corner
Leap across pages and tape
One more song it's not to late
U2 moves the crowd
"Stuck in a Moment"
And what I would give
To be in that moment
Fly to Neverland with Walt himself
Find his swing, Redford's Legend of Bagger
Explore Tolkien's caves, the dwarves did delve
With Indy Jones the Last Crusader
To save the planet, ultimate plan conceived
Mission Impossible is achieved

To be stuck in that moment
When the sun drowns my eyes
That moment
When the pictures on my wall

Come alive...

Emilyn Edquilang
Grade 10, Morse High
Poet-teacher: Glory Foster
Teacher: Cynthia Larkin

THE WORST PART OF THE DAY

When I wake up in the morning
I feel like frozen yogurt
like a cracked egg.
I'm as cranky as a black crow.

When I wake up in the morning
I feel like someone stapled my head
to a radio that blares loud music.

I feel as stiff as a statue
sculpted a million years ago.

When I wake up in the morning
it feels like a pit bull bit my leg
then dragged me into the hot sun.

Sulekha Mohamud
Grade 5, Marshal Elementary
Poet-teacher: Johnnierenee Nelson
Teacher: John Bartholomew

Flashes of Family

My sister is a cat.
She grooms herself with care.
Picking out carefully the best fur for the day.
"Shall I be tabby?" she asks,
"Or perhaps,
Calico, though I like HER striking shade of orange.
Oh Mamaaaaa, what do you think?"
She cuddles like a kitten,
Sitting sweetly on your lap.
Purrrrring purrring "Can you read me a book pleeaaase?"
Looking at you with big round eyes.
She plays quietly in her room
With her ball of string,
Basking in the sunshine.

My brother is a hummingbird
He **flashes** to
         and fro
            and to
               and fro.
Always active, *flitting* about
He turns on a dime
From weeping to laughter—
Like a light switch
        ON!!
He will zoooom
Until suddenly
He.
Stops.

My mother is a checklist,
There is always something to do.
People to see
Places to go
Dishes
Laundry
School
Always on the go.
Her whole life is written down somewhere,
In tedius monotony

Elizabeth Nichols
Grade 10, Heritage Christian
Poet-teacher: Jill Moses
Teacher: Mary Jane Najor

"Early November" by Andrew Manalo / Morse High

THE HANDS OF THE HEART

My Mom's hands are soft as a bird
They move as fast as a bunny
Her nails are short and
She has a V-shape in her palm
They look like snow
Falling from the big blue sky
Sometimes they move very slowly
When they're tired
From working so hard
Then she folds her bird hands
Floating in the sky
soft and slow

Zenia Motta
Grade 3, Las Palmas Elementary
Poet-teacher: Glory Foster
Teacher: Mary Ann Wheatly

"These Hands" by Ben Johnston / Mesa Verde Middle

THE DEPRESSION OF MY HANDS

I feel
the dancing anger
living on my exploding fingertips
with forgiveness trying
hard, hard to escape with
a single flash.
I feel
selfishness thundering out
as my fiery hands float in the shadows of
danger and depression.
No laughter.
No care.
Just dangerous.

Kelsey Elling
Grade 5, Dingeman Elementary
Poet-teacher: Veronica Cunningham
Teacher: Rochelle Schwartz

THE HISTORY OF MY MASKS

Innocence? HA!
My sister stole that mask from me
but it's too small for her head
because her demon horns poke through the top.

So I had to get a new mask.

First, I tried my brother's mask.
He's a lot older than me, so it fit for a long time.
But as time passed, that mask grew small too.
His mask no longer fit like I wanted it to.

Next, I tried my dad's mask...big mistake.
It was too scratchy (I think a few whiskers got stuck in it.)
It was too old and heavy for my head,
the eye slits were too small, no one could see inward.

So I tried my mom's mask...too soft.
It was like wet clay and molded too much to my face.
Plus, it was totally the wrong colors for me,
they washed me out, her skin tone's lighter than mine.

Now I have my own mask, a compilation of the others.
Innocent like my sister's
big on me like my brother's
bulky and thick and secretive like my dad's
darker versions of the colors of my mom's.
My mask fits perfectly, it's uniquely configured for me.

Alexis Norausky
Grade 12, Morse High
Poet-teacher: Glory Foster
Teacher: Jeff Meyer

LONELINESS

Loneliness is a dark hole
in the pocket of a young boy
sitting on a bench in the rain.
Smelling of musty carpet,
it drains through every soul
and creeps into every heart.
But it shows us how to appreciate
the warmth of family and friends.

Ashley Payton
Grade 5, Jerabek Elementary
Poet-teacher: Celia Sigmon
Teacher: Phyllis Collins

"Loneliness" by Christina Bertrang / Morse High

WOMAN

inspired by O'Keeffe's "Inside Red Canna"

Fiery hot red
your shades and colors
don't account for all of your facets.
The depths of your mind
are unsearchable;
your colorful hues are infinite.
Sharp edges cut
as I lightly pass by
but your feathery skin
soothes and replenishes me.
Flaunt your colors like a mating peacock
such innocence and fragility.
Your curves sway
as the wind blows through.
The glow that radiates from you
shows the passion
the power
that you have
Woman.

Lori Alvarado
Grade 12, Morse High
Poet-teacher: Glory Foster
Teacher: Jeff Meyer

"Curves" by Jose Hernandez / Morse High

A Sight To See

inspired by Thomas Surijo

In the front of a theater sits a man
Who made going to movies feel so grand
His name is Chaplin small and petite
And to his left sits someone so sweet
Her name is Temple first child star
At the age of seven she bought her own car
    So many people in just one frame
    I feel like I am playing a Hollywood game
To the left of Temple is Howard Duff
Who made going to movies feel so tough
So many credits in his repertoire
Third row back sits a star
His name is Allen glasses and all
He is tiny but ability makes him tall
    So many people in just one frame
    I feel I am playing a Hollywood game
Enough with humans, lets go surreal
With a character that'll make girls squeal
A cartoon character by the name of Woody
So many laughs in just one showing
    So many people in just one frame
    I feel I am playing a Hollywood game

Cooper Smith
Grade 7, Mesa Verde Middle
Poet-teacher: Glory Foster
Teacher: David Sykes

VARIETIES OF SMOOTH

Smooth is the shell of an unblemished egg.
It is the shine of the sea at night.
Smooth is quiet.
It is as quiet as morning.
Smooth is a bird that has been in the rain.
It is my slippers resting in front of the fireplace.
Smooth is a ballerina that gracefully flies through the air.
It is an orchestra preparing for a performance.
Smooth is an angel that has gained her wings.
It is a silk bookmark lodged in the corners of history.
Smooth is the gentle breeze that shakes a tree.
It is a fairy that is waving "good-bye."
It is a dusty book on the top shelf; a story that has not yet been told.
Smooth is a gentle oak leaf falling, falling to the ground.

Anna Najor
Grade 6, Heritage Christian
Poet-teacher: Jill Moses
Teacher: Mary Jane Najor

"Symentry of Opposites" by Steven Xu / Mesa Verde Middle

Another Game, an Epilogue?

Writing is a game of chess
Not to be hurried.
Each sentence should be pondered
Like the next move.
The pawns are your words
Ready at your call.
And the king dominates all
Just as the author rules his fiction universe.
Writer's block is a temporary halt
A check that could soon become checkmate.
A tentative move, a knight
—does the paragraph fit?
The threat is gone, and the game continues.
Study the board, make adjustments
The story must have the proper end.
The bishop moves closer as the plot thickens
Tension builds as the climax draws near.
Study the paper, ready your move
One more rook, a knight, a paragraph, a line
One more sentence, and then...
"Checkmate"
The story is finished...

Kristina Flavier
Grade 8, Stanley Middle
Poet-teacher: Glory Foster
Teacher: Reissa Schrager-Cole

JOY

Joy is a feeling
of peace and excitement
all at the same time.
Joy is the feeling
when I am reading a book
on a rainy day
in front of a crackling fire
taking sips of hot chocolate.

Joy is the feeling
when I am galloping bareback
on an ebony mare
across an open meadow.
Joy lives in a library;
she comes in and out of the shelves,
and dances around
inside a book waiting
to be read.

Joy is the feeling
when I bite
into a freshly baked apple pie.
The melted sugar wraps around my tongue
like a silk ribbon
inviting me to eat more.
Joy plays on a rainbow;
she reminds me of the promise
of hope after a storm.

Joy is the exciting feeling
when a mother bird teaches
her chicks to fly.
They look uncertain,
but with a bit of faith tucked under their wings
their hopes soar.

Meghan O'Brien
Grade 6, Heritage Christian
Poet-teacher: Jill Moses
Teacher: Laurie O'Brien

"Home Sweet Home" by Samantha Mauro / Mesa Verde Middle

ARMOR FIT FOR A KNIGHT

My shield of quick wit will feign any unwanted
attack of insults.
I'm rubber and you are glue, you know.
Sticks and Stones, you know.
Words can never hurt me.
My breastplate of excuses will turn
any blade of responsibility.
The dog ate it, you know.
It was an accident, you know.
I swear to God!
My helmet of confidence will protect
my vulnerable insecurity.
I can run faster than you, you know.
I am more talented than you, you know.
Anything you can do, I can do better.
My piercing blade of company will stab
the heart of everything else.
No more will I be alone.
No more will I be excluded.
I will be treated like the noblest knight from now on.

Daniel Tostado
Grade 9, Patrick Henry High
Poet-teacher: Veronica Cunningham
Teacher: Linda Good

"SAY CHEESE! 1...2...3..CLICK"

If I were a camera
I'd capture time with a push of a button
I would taste the sweetness
Of your happiness with a single click
Or see the darkness of a sad farewell
Brightened with a flash
If I were a camera
I'd hear you laugh cry or count to three
Or be focused with a gentle touch
Of your hands
I would be able to see
Your memories frozen in time
Memories of a Happy Birthday
Or a Merry Christmas
If I were a camera
I'd be your life captured and frozen
With just a single click...

Maelihini Adamos
Grade 10, Morse High
Poet-teacher: Glory Foster
Teacher: Cynthia Larkin

Rainbow Family

I am a chameleon.
At school I am quiet
I am gold.
At home I am a loud
green forest, when I'm angry
a red chili pepper.

My brother Ricky is a rock.
He doesn't let anything in.
He is a heavy boulder when he hits me.

My brother Danny is a bright spider.
Sometimes I just want to squish him.

My mom is a colorful heart
gold when she is happy
blue wqhen she's frustrated
black when she is angry
red when she's loving
yellow when she is having fun.

My dad is a tree with a woodpecker
perched on it, working on the weekdays.
On the weekends he's relaxed
and sleeps like a dead branch.

My dog is like a teddy bear
cuddled up with a baby.
            GOOD NIGHT!

Sarah Toothacre
Grade 7, Longfellow Middle
Poet-teacher: Johnnierenee Nelson
Teacher: Sarah Karp

THE COLOR OF AN ANSEL ADAMS PHOTOGRAPH

The contrast between Black and White
Summarizes the pages of words
Inspired by the colors of autumn
It captures the brittle uneven surface
Of a red maple leaf
Its surfaces of hills and valleys
And its rouge stem of unmalleable wire
The leaf's infrastructure
A series of fibers holding it together
Becomes a river delta at sunset
As it is blown off its branch
And across a glistening lake
Its odyssey captured
And summarized in shades of Gray.

Melanie Enriquez
Grade 11, Morse High
Poet-teacher: Glory Foster
Teacher: Jeff Meyer

"Black & White World" by Lawrence Whitfield / Morse High

ODE TO THE PEN

It is with this black knife
That I rip through the walls of this room.
It is with this dark scepter
That I cast my spells upon this desk.
A cataclysmic tool
That carves away at the stone of my heart
Chipping away at the facade
Unleashing the fury caged inside.
> The oceans dry
> Mountains explode
> The sun dims
> And the stars fall down
When my hand meets the pen
Meeting the paper.
With this divine rod
I traverse the Earth and Sky.
With this magic dagger
I stab at Life and Death.
With this black pen
I can determine all fates.
It is my world
And everything else
Is a puppet in my play.

Mikhael Andaya
Grade 12, Morse High
Poet-teacher: Glory Foster
Teacher: Jeff Meyer

"All Around the World" by Brianne Sheeny / Mesa Verde Middle

MY TRIBE

My dad is soil, the earth
Often we step on him, ignoring his existence
Yet he is the very ground beneath our feet
When we start to wither, he enriches us with himself

My mom is a violet hat
When the brim is up, light and happiness
When it is down, harshness and tears
Yet she shades us all

Ethan, a radio that is always on
His life a constant song of noise and excitement
We plug our ears, then strangely miss his songs

His constant companion, Spencer, a stormy blue bird
With one wing broken, bleeding
He soars for the sky and comes crashing down
He pecks us, for his heart is breaking
Yet one day he will soar above us all

And I am a blade of grass
Growing in the fertile earth shaded by a violet hat
A living breathing green, fresh and innocent
Yet a blade of grass can slice a threatening hand
Though stomped on, it springs back up
Always I am reaching for the sky

Kylee Danielson
Grade 11, Heritage Christian
Poet-teacher: Jill Moses
Teacher: Joyce Danielson

"The Wind Blows"
by Brandon M. Luzano / Morse High

DON'T YOU SEE?

Don't you see?
At school,
Shields are up.
Every day from seven to two,
We hide
Even among friends.

Don't you see
The difficulty of a good poem?
To reveal enough to be "real"
Is to risk exactly what we work all day to avoid:
Utter embarrassment.
The word must be just right
Not "too" anything.
Not too serious, not trying too hard to be funny
Not too emotional, not pretentious
Not too personal, not phony
Not too teacher-pleasing
But pleasing enough for everyone.
In other words,
Perfect.

Don't you see?
Even the popular elite
Pretending
Maybe more than anyone else.
Today, punks sit in a perfect row
Matching black t-shirts
Bobbing spiked heads in unison
Listening to "Fat Lip":
"I don't want to be
A casualty of society."
Who sees the irony?
We don't want to be trapped
In this web of pretending
But it's survival
And we're mostly happy
Until we have to write poetry.
Don't you see how much you're asking?

Naomi Geraci
Grade 8, Standley Middle
Poet-teacher: Veronica Cunningham
Teacher: Sharon Nold

"The Rose of Pestilence" by Alvin C. Vintayen / Morse High

BLACK IS A SMACK

Black is a smack on the cheek
that a bully at school gives me.
First it turns purple, then blue, then black.
I hate black. It feels like something
creeping up my back
in the middle of the night,
like the ocean, chilly and cold.
Black is sad. It reminds me of death.
It has no pleasant thoughts
and feels like hairy spider legs.
When I'm cooped up inside
on a dark winter day, black is weights
that are holding me down.
Black is a smack, a fear as dark as a hole
I fell into, where I'm trapped in black.

Julia Burns
Grade 5, Jerabek Elementary
Poet-teacher: Celia Sigmon
Teacher: Kathie Lloyd

"Falling into Place" by Ryan Caganap / Morse High

A BAD SCHOOL DAY

Walk into class
sit chat
listen for bell
Science
sit listen learn
chat chat chat
referral
walk to office
call parents
chat
listen listen listen
hang up
go to lunch
eat drink
avoid trouble
and geeks
P. E.
dress
run sit stretch
run play
dress again
Art
sit listen draw
chat chat chat
referral
call parents
listen
hang up
Home
sit listen
listen listen listen
Grounded...

Jordan McKinney
Grade 8, Stanley Middle
Poet-teacher: Glory Foster
Teacher: Reissa Schrager-Cole

Ode to the computer (not working)

It hums like a monk
making you smile.
You put in the floppy
and open the program,
but then it happens
like a storm
crashing on the hull.
The floppy pushes out
sticks a tongue at you.
Frantically, you hit the buttons
like a search for the lifeboat that isn't there.
You know what happens next
like the ancients knew
what happened to those who
got lost in the Labyrinth.
It tells you to wait
like a siren tells
you to wander closer.
You know there is no
time left, the ship is
sinking, the minotaur
is coming
and the death of the hum
is as loud as the wreck
hitting the bottom.

Max Thompson
Grade 8, San Pasqual Union
Poet-teacher: Jill Moses
Teacher: Michael de Neve

"The Storm" by Sammy B. Sotoa / Morse High

"Expansion" by Michael Angelo M. Paz / Morse High

JUST LINES

These are just lines.
Lines that scratch and cut glass.
Squish between toes
Lines blinding the eyes.
These are just lines
Lines carrying bodies
On their muscular shoulders.
Connecting you to people
On the outside world.
Lines causing land to erode.
These are just lines.
Lines that warm the unclothed
Spreading glittering specks of light
Across the ocean.
Lines that burn and sting.
No, these aren't just lines.

Irish-Joyce Diwa
Grade 9, Morse High
Poet-teacher: Glory Foster
Teacher: Carol Zupkas

"Cool Dude" by Melissa Corona / Southwest Middle

INVISIBLE HAT

As clean as paper,
as indestructible as God,
when I put my invisible hat on
I feel like a ghost,
as foggy as the midnight moon,
as cool as a breeze.
It makes me different
because I can fly.
It makes me as smart as Einstein.

Joseph Ceceña IV
Grade 4, Lincoln Acres Elementary
Poet-teacher: Celia Sigmon
Teacher: Lisa Scott

HISTORY HAT

When I have trouble with homework
or even a story to write,
I put on my thinking cap and think.
I feel the colors change every time:
canary yellow or desperate pink,
sorrow blue or silent green.
It tells me all the answers
before I even ask the questions.
It moves my brain so gently,
making me think of slavery,
dinasours and even t.v.
It makes me agitated instead of stressed.
It tells words in Latin and even Chinese.
But tell me in English, please, please, please.

Sara Johnson
Grade 4, Jerabek Elementary
Poet-teacher: Celia Sigmon
Teacher: Angela Tucker

A Prison of Uncooked Meat or Frog Legs

School is...
A prison with no escape
A building without windows
Angry teachers
Bossy principals
Missing homework
Bad grades
Upset parents
Short lunches
Long lines
Disgusting food
Food fights
Bird poop falling from the sky
Warm chairs, cold stares
Screaming, crazy chattering
Groups of friends
Gossip
Passing notes
Gum under tables
Detention passes
Crowded hallways
Roller backpacks tripping everyone
Big bullies, little victims
Boring never-ending lessons
Gray and beige walls
Mustard carpets
Naive substitute ·
Funny pranks
Cut up frogs
And chicken legs
Forever lasting days
Locked inside
Lost hope of escaping

Christina Buckley
Grade 8, Stanley Middle
Poet-teacher: Glory Foster
Teacher: Ressia Schrager-Cole

*"A Ruined Puzzel" by Mikael Cabal /
Morse High*

ODE TO MY TEACHER

My teacher is as nice as
a cup of lemonade in the Sahara
as tall as a mountain
as shorts as an ant.
Her smile is as big
as a clown's laugh.
Sweet,
yet witty.
Gentle,
yet strict.
We love her
and she loves us.
Her hair is as brown
As a sip of hot chocolate
in the morning.
Stylish,
Simple,
Sparkling,
These all describe her personality.
As pretty as a blue daisy:
my teacher,
my classroom,
my class.
When I talk to her I feel like flying deeper, deeper
deeper into space.

Tara Mullally
Grade 6, Del Mar Heights Elementary
Poet-teacher: Jill Moses
Teacher: Keri Gibson

The Torture That Was My Life

I was angry with blood red eyes
unable to protect my family
life always changing
swirling, swerving
people never stopping to listen
or understand.

These days people have no respect for others
I tried to change that.
I dreamt of a life where people
no matter what color, race
language or gang would be equal.

No, I don't miss my body.
Why would I miss getting locked
up in jail, beaten with chains, billy clubs
getting shot with guns, seeing my people
chased by dogs?

Why would I miss all that
torture from white people—
the crowbars, the water hoses?
Now I can roam free, can talk and be with
great and powerful African kings.

Desiree Trejo
Grade 7, Longfellow Academy
Poet-teacher: Johnnierenee Nelson
Teacher: Sarah Karp

A Day in the Life of a Barbie Doll

Barbie strolls over to her red convertible and rolls
the top down. The car sputters to life
and saunters along the
beige carpet
with the help
of
sweaty human hands.
Barbie pops her fluorescent pink gum
and
turns up the volume
on the radio.
Heavy metal music
blares through the microscopic speakers.
Barbie jumps out of the car
and ambles
to a
clothing store.
Coming out,
she is dressed
in punk clothing,
the new sensation.
The newspaper headlines scream,
"Punk Rocker Barbie on sale NOW!!!!"
Barbie sighs and disappears into the
power hungry
paparazzi.

Morgan Golumbuk
Grade 6, Lewis Middle
Poet-teacher: Jana Gardner
Teacher: Jamie Walsh

Dancing Dirt Bikes

Dirt bikes leap, fly like helicopters
across muddy ramps

dirt bikes zoom
blur red, yelllow, blue

some have stripes like American flags
others have spots like cheetahs

all streak by with black two-digit numbers.

Jose Peña
Grade 3, Central Elementary
Poet-teacher: Johnnierenee Nelson
Teacher: Delia Robinson

"Le Tour" by Tiffany Geronimo / Morse High

Loss of an Already Confused Mind

Packing up my exhausted life
Forced to throw 15 years into an empty box.
Seems hauntingly small
Can't fit everything
So I just give up.
Oh, no!
Where's my sanity?

I must have lost her in the moment.

Running around
Trying anxiously to
Piece myself back together
But I can't find the super glue.

I am starting to feel lonely
My whole life compacted
Into this one hectic day.
Where am I?

A lost flame in the fire
Burning to be found.
It hurts to be this lost.

Brianna Serrano
Grade 9, Patrick Henry High
Poet-teacher: Veronica Cunningham
Teacher: Linda Good

MAD FIRES

I see the reddish roaring fires
forcing the weak houses to cry aloud.
I see the dark sky dying and wanting to survive
helped by the rain.
I see the Bernadino Ranch burning rapidly in flames.
I see horses dying and burning.
I see people scared and taking care of their families.
I see them.

Brenda Coronel
Grade 6, Kimball Elementary
Poet-teacher: Francisco Bustos
Teacher: Beneranda J. Calderon

"Devil's Wrath" by Khristinne Bituin / Morse High

CHILD BORN OF FLAMES

The child born of flames,
kindled by its passion for life
stretched its long fingers
to grasp the brittle brush for food.
Gorging on life to satisfy its own.
The more it tastes the dry grasses and trees, the more it
grows.
More powerful than the sea, but just as unpredictable.
Finally, reaching its maximum potential,
the life that had grown fought valiantly and died.
So misunderstood by many.
People think of terror and destruction
when they imagine such fires.
That the bright orange spirit
that has cleared our land is a monster.
The sizzling flame is not so different from us, though.
Like us, it started as a child and died at old age.

Sara Rode
Grade 8, Greenfield Middle
Poet-teacher: Jill Moses
Teacher: Dina Sterner

THE WIND AND WAR

Listen to the wind, it speaks to you
Telling of disastrous wars
Hear the wind, it speaks to you
Shouting, screaming, sounds of gunfire
Smell the wind, it brushes past you
Smoke everywhere, the smell
Of dead bodies rotting away
Feel the wind, it touches you
The coldness of dead flesh, open wounds
Blood dripping from your fingers
Taste the wind, it feeds you
The taste of gunpowder,
Hunger in their empty stomachs
See the wind, it shows you
The dying, the wounded
The brave men who fight on
Listen to the wind, it speaks to you
In the clatter of cottonwood trees
Like machine gun fire on a battlefield...

Amanda Deguia
Grade 10, Morse High
Poet-teacher: Glory Foster
Teacher: Mary Scanlon

"The Message" by Joselito Matundan / Morse High

THE AMERICAN FLAG

The fifty states look like a piece of the sky
folded into a tiny square.
I can hear it standing strong for freedom.
It smells like fresh air on a full-moon night
and tastes like peach cobbler.
Thousands of hands reach for it.
I will try my hardest
to keep my country free.

Ashlee Ruff
Grade 4, Jerabek Elementary
Poet-teacher: Celia Sigmon
Teacher: Christina Martin

WAR'S ACT

Bam! The shot of a gun.
A war waking up.
Each side is returning fire.
It is a scary, painful, bloody,
and brutal act.
One man down, then another.
Hostages or none, still a
pitiful scene.
The sun goes down, the
moon comes up, but
the war continues.

Spencer Beaulieu
Grade 5, San Pasqual Union
Poet-teacher: Paula Jones
Teachers: Wendy Snapp and Karalee Gorham

"American Corruption in the 21st Century"
by Lendl San Jose / Morse High

Taking a Potshot

"Potshot," a very casual word
Or a very casual shot
Borrowed from Middle English, "to shoot"
But now we use it for easy targets
Perhaps when they took potshots at soldiers
Now we take them at bottles.

Potshots are like my random thoughts
Shots launched into the darkness
Not knowing whether they hit their mark or not
It's unclear
Like the bombs we drop
Or the wars we've fought
Or the bullets we've shot
The truths we've sought
All potshots in the darkness.

Potshot long ago was invented by old wives
In the darkness they'd hear the mouse squeak
In the darkness they'd hurl the pot
No longer were the targets noble
Or the throw calculated.
It was as simple as
Taking a potshot.

Andrie V. Spondonis
Grade 10, Morse High
Poet-teacher: Glory Foster
Teacher: Mary Scanlon

LOVE AND HATE

"Paper Heart" by Andrew Manalo / Morse High

BAKERSFIELD & YOUR LETTERS IN THE MORNING

You wrote me
letters
that the sun slipped through my window
at 7:00 AM

and told me of moist November leaves
huddled together in piles
at the edge of the street
as if they attempted to keep warm
from the cold air whispering
your name
through barren cotton fields.
And it sang
a song
composed
     of jeweled monarch wings
     dancing grasshoppers
     singing slingshots
     and sticky strawberry ice cream melted on the curb.
They remained the intangible
letters
that collected in the lonely crevasses of my mind
playing back in slow motion
until the last leaf fell...
Then I realized
I would have to step beyond your
foggy
dew kissed mornings
and understand that there was
a world
beyond
your endless grapevines.

Dorothy Manimtim
Grade 11, Morse High
Poet-teacher: Glory Foster
Teacher: Jeff Meyer

KISSING

It tastes like spit
and feels slobbery and wet.
You hear nothing
but there's love in the air,
and it is face to face.
Romance helps,
but it takes love to do.

Matthew Steiger
Grade 5, Jerabek Elementary
Poet-teacher: Celia Sigmon
Teacher: Jean Chalupsky

"Love" by Allison Han / Mesa Verde Middle

Twisted Licorice Emotions

A kiss is like riding a roller coaster
Once your lips touch you're buckled in
For a ride of love
Where your feelings spiral down
Into the pit of your stomach
And rise to the top once again
Your heart pumps wildly as this ride takes you
Through the loops and fast turns
Where your feelings are twisted like licorice
On the ride of love
You overflow with joy and emotion
And when the ride is over
You'll be begging for more
Desiring to recapture
The feeling you adore...

Tanika Anderson-Bailey
Grade 10, Morse High School
Poet-teacher: Glory Foster
Teacher: Cynthia Larkin

WORDS OF THE HEART

The students, intent on their work
bend over their papers
scribbling furiously, feverishly
as epiphanies hit them.
The muses descend among them
giving them inspiration
putting fire into their pencils.
Ideas bombard them.
It's war, as the kids hurry
to catch the thoughts
before they drift away.
Ideas bright, colorful ideas
caught in the mind
like butterflies in a net.
Those ideas are unleashed
on the paper
as powerful as lightening bolts
to strike readers dumb with astonishment.
These words have the ability
to make the reader cry,
laugh or feel good inside.
The passion of
Poetry.

Sarah Claytor
Grade 7, Mesa Verde Middle
Poet-teacher: Glory Foster
Teacher: Marycay Densmore

Thirteen

Red, black, green, white, twirling and whirling into my
soul, they are a whirlpool, sucking in the loves of my life.
The bangs, beats, silence, and strums, the endless worlds
I imagine, falling in an endless spiral. A silent unknown
predator lurks in the darkness, pouncing on the swirls of
lights. Flashes, beeps, hums and whirrs, thousands of
sounds forming an abstract musicale, all watched by a
silent presence without eyes, listening without ears.
Pops, bangs, flashes, whirls, billions of colors folding
into one shape, arms,
legs, nose and hair,
Me.

Matthew Paulson
Grade 8, Lewis Middle
Poet-teacher: Jana Gardner
Teacher: Kathryn Dominique

"Odd One Out" by Sarah Crow / Canyon View Elementary

THE RED ROAD

Red is my color
for walking the Red Road.
It is what my ancestors
believed in.
It shows me
what comes next in life.
The Red Road is love
and I wish the whole world
was full of this kind
of love.

Kyle Davalos
Grade 3, Jacumba Elementary
Poet-teacher: Celia Sigmon
Teacher: Susan Barry

DANCING WITH COLOR

Messy fingers
Squish together.
Sky blue meets cherry red.
A muddy purple
Splatters like grape rain
On the budding masterpiece.
A stream of blood red
Whirls onto the marvelous mess.
Royal blue, flamingo pink
A tempting puddle forms.
Lime green fingers
Waltz through the rainbow ooze.
Hands tango in hypnotic swirls.
Stop to comtemplate.
Painted palm to chubby cheek
A memory left.

A smile spreads
Loves the feel of cool color,
Squirts sunshine
Onto pink puffy knees.
Midnight black drips
Peppering a once clean shirt.
Excitement rises.
Tangerine orange explodes on a nearby wall.
Smile widens
A new dance begins.

Maddy Bersin
Grade 6, Hawthorne Elementary
Poet-teacher: Veronica Cunningham
Teacher: Tricia Smith

Solo Tú Sabes

Cuando estás triste,
me siento mal.
Cuando estás alegre,
me siento feliz.

¿Pero sabes qué es
lo que me hace más
feliz?

Saber que eres mi mamá.

Tus ojos me reflejan cuando
debo seguir,
tu boca cuando debo hablar,
y tu corazón cuando te debo amar.

"Lost Feelings" by Arlene Dacio / Morse High

ONLY YOU KNOW

When you are sad,
I feel bad.
When you are happy,
I feel joy.

But do you know what
makes me feel the
happiest?

Knowing that you are my mother.

Your eyes signal to me
when I should continue,
your mouth when I should speak,
and your heart when I should love.

Yesenia Sánchez Acosta
Age 15, Casa-Hogar Lirio de los Valles Tijuana
Poet-teacher: Francisco Bustos
Director: Sara Duña

ODE TO RED CRAYON

Her hair is
glossy and bright
running around the lined
slate unable to control
the urge to race from
left to right.
She stands out of
the crowd dotting
the page
to show her love.
The beautiful red
lips engulf the
white nothingness.
She was made from
scraps of sunbeams,
raindrops and anger
and now is becoming
shorter from the
hands of love that
use her and her life.

Taylor Phillips
Grade 8, San Pasqual Union
Poet-teacher: Jill Moses
Teacher: Michael de Neve

THE DREAM

Pokey red bursts through my mind
like evil thorns as dark as death.
In the background I can hear
jumping cholla whispering in my ear.
They tell me how the thorns
spear the red. As I listen
I understand how love never tries to die,
how killing fire burns the bad.
While lush green yells and shouts,
all is a blur. Then I hear a voice.
"Wake up, wakeup, Sweety Pie."

Rebecca E. Billman
Grade 3, Hearst Elementary
Poet-teacher: Celia Sigmon
Teacher: Jean Feinstein

"No Way, Go Away"
by Sabra Cheshire / Valley Vista Elementary

A WOMAN'S SILK WHITE DRESS IN A WINDY MEADOW

after a painting by Rafal Olbinski

Her silky egg white dress
as if a cloud
not yet darkened by rain.
Her hair is blown back
like feathers of a bird in flight.
It's getting very windy
while the sea of darkness
rolling in the sky deepens.
The bird's eye is
a pool of poppies growing
in a meadow.
In this meadow, time has no meaning.
The poppies are swaying like
a snake in a trance.
The wind is a cool breeze
like a baby taking its first step
or saying its
first word.

Shealyn Brake
Grade 8, San Pasqual Union
Poet-teacher: Jill Moses
Teacher: Michael de Neve

ARTIST WITH MONKEYS
inspired by Frida Kahlo

Hideously Beautiful
furry little animals, black and white
tropical oasis, brownish green
exotic orange plant
But wait,
a woman with monkeys hung around her neck
seems so ugly,
yet so wonderful.

A strange woman she seems to be
eyebrows like bushes
hair like night.
Mexican woman
please, tell me
why so ugly,
when so beautiful.
Through our eyes she is not gorgeous.
Through our hearts
she's so beautiful.
In my mind, I try to see,
why so ugly,
when really there's nothing wrong
she just feels her looks are a major problem.
To me she is perfect.
She is a hideously beautiful woman
with a love of monkeys.

Bianca Manriquez
Grade 7, Southwest Middle
Poet-teacher: Glory Foster
Teacher: Pat Koob

Yo Soy un Piano Que Agarra el Alma y el Amor

Yo soy un piano que agarra el alma y el amor.
Yo soy una flauta que canta como noche de paz,
y siento los sentimientos de las personas que buscan
algo increíble.

Yo soy una guitarra que vive en el bosque y veo peces
volando en el cielo.
Yo soy un violín que canta, y se laboran por mí,
y estoy gorda para que todos canten y hablen de mí.

Yo soy un tambor muy feliz.
Yo soy una maraca y me gusta tocar la música rápida,
y entiendo
que todos me tocan a mí porque soy hermosa.

Yo soy un arpa que duerme a personas
y hablo de mis amigos, y brillo mis ojos.

Yo soy un saxofón, y hago mucho ruido.

Yo soy una trompeta muy feliz y ando
por el pasto buscando algo que necesito.

Yo soy una ardilla que busca un acordeón
para tocarte una música de amor.

"Music" by Patrick Eria / Morse High

I Am a Piano That Grabs the Soul and Love

I am a piano that grabs the soul and love.
I am a flute that sings like it's a holy night,
and I feel the emotions of people seeking something
incredible.

I am a guitar that lives in the jungle, and I can see fish
flying in the sky.
I am a violin that sings, and people work for me,
and I am very happy that everybody can sing and talk
about me.

I am a very happy drum.
I am a maraca, and I like to play fast music,
and I understand
that everybody plays me because I am beautiful.

I am a harp that soothes people to sleep
and I speak of my friends, and I shine my eyes.

I am saxophone, and I make a lot of noise.

I am a happy trumpet and I am moving
through the grass, searching for what I need.

I am a squirrel in search for an accordion
to play music of love.

Viviana Zapata Carrillo
Age 12, Aldea Infantil SOS Tijuana
Poet-teacher: Francisco Bustos
Director: Luis Manuel Reza

Heaven Itself

I am white like heaven itself,
like a cloud, as clear as a rain drop
falling from the sky,
as beautiful as a soaring angel.
In fall, I fly like the white dove of peace,
as white as the great light of the sun
shining through the huge oak trees.

Arissa Rodriguez
Grade 4, Lincoln Acres
Poet-teacher: Celia Sigmon
Teacher: Lisa Scott

Peace

Peace is a dove in flight
      and the stillness of a bear in winter
Peace is rain drizzling upon your face
      the dew falling from a leaf
Peace is the softness of snow
      and the sweetness of berries
Peace is the sound of music
      or the sleeping kitten by the fireplace
Peace is the scent of lilies in spring
      and the leaves rustling in autumn
Peace is cotton candy melting in your mouth
      or a message of love
      and silence in a bottle...

Jolene Xie
Grade 7, Mesa Verde Middle
Poet-teacher: Glory Foster
Teacher: David Sykes

"Happy but Sad" by Marcos Quirós / Southwest Middle

ANGER

Red fire in the woods
the screeches and squawks of rabbits
birds, large cats and snakes
trying to escape the flames

Anger
burnt bread
tears of red roses
rising like steam in a coffee pot.

Jessica Yidi
Grade 5, Valley Vista Elementary
Poet-teacher: Johnnierenee Nelson
Teacher: Mary Guzman

PEACE

Peace is a relaxing feeling, like sipping warm hot chocolate on a cold winter day.
Peace is feeling relieved that the day's tasks are over.
Peace comes in a bright-eyed puppy gazing at you nose to nose.
Peace comes when taking off your slippers right before you say your nightly prayers.
Peace is a feeling that comes when relaxing in a hot bath filled to the brim with scented oils.
Peace is a feeling when you are asleep, and know someone is taking care of you the rest of your days.
Peace comes when a woman is gracefully sliding her pen on canvas to make wonders.

Katherine Najor
Grade 6, Heritage Christian
Poet-teacher: Jill Moses
Teacher: Mary Jane Najor

"Sailing in Paradise" by Vanessa Frigillana / Morse High

PEACE

I am the friend of respect and loyalty,
The sister of love and hope.
I am the sea's gentle waves and the
Land's refreshing breeze.
War and violence hate me
And friendship and joy love me.
I am the soft sound of a flute and I
occur before and after wars.
I am peace.

Jamaica Adviento
Grade 7, Greenfield Middle
Poet-teacher: Georgette James
Teacher: Emily Sabin

FOOD FOR THOUGHT

"A Night in Paris" by Claudine Samson / Morse High

POETRY IS...

Poetry is
a
 ripe,
  red,
   juicy
    apple
    that
     cheers
    me
up,
 making
 me
  dream
 of
  anything
 I
want.

Esteban Venegas
Grade 5, John Marshall Elementary
Poet-teacher: Jana Gardner
Teacher: Leslie Johnson

GREATEST MEAL EVER

I go to a restaurant.
I order poetry with paper and pencils.
I start with the pencils.
Ugh...
Then the paper.
Ugh...
But the poetry had a certain taste.
The taste of . . .
Well, I really can't explain it.
All I can say is
It's like nothing I've ever had.
It was the taste of everything
I've ever had and more.
When it first entered my mouth,
I just wanted to scarf the rest down.
Every culture, state, country
In one little meal.

Billy Slane
Grade 3, St. Patrick's School
Poet-teacher: Jill Moses
Teacher: Brenda Sasso

ODE TO WASABI

It walks into my dish
side by side with its best friend: shoyu.
I stir it in
chopsticks in hand.
It dissolves as fast as
water evaporates in the outback of Australia
in summer.
Sashimi wouldn't be the same without it.
Having sushi without wasabi
would be like
earth without any water in sight.
It spices up my dinner
as music spices up a party.
Take too much and your nose will turn.
But take too little and you'll miss out on the excitement.
Wasabi is the key
to Japan.

Katie Kobayashi
Grade 5, St. Patrick's School
Poet-teacher: Jill Moses
Teacher: Anne Kramer

"Shadow of Love & Fun" by Heather Hatfield
Canyon View Elementary

Vanilla extract

Fresh morning, like wind, a chemical, summer and fall
mixed, almost evening time, sunsets, liquid, all rich
candy mixed and melted, sweet, unusual eating, some-
thing by a warm fire at night, a chilly night, it makes me
sleepy, chess, a deli, wonderful seasonings and spices
mixed, frost, a cat on your lap, fuzzy things, warm cozy
clouds, log cabins, wet old old straw hats, Christmas
treats, Easter joy, oak trees, April, baking in the sun,
it makes you relax, Aunt Nancy's sweet kitchen, a
waterfall, Thanksgiving with Tiana David and Buddy
(a dog) who looks like a wild wolf, a soft light or a kind
of mist in the window, making holiday goodies with
mom, decorating the tree at Christmas, hanging the
stockings, gazing out the window, cinnamon.

Kristina Deusch
Grade 7, Tri-City Christian Homeschool
Poet-teacher: Jill Moses
Teacher: Darlene Deusch

ODE TO COFFEE

Oh sweet elixir, touch my lips again!
I've known no kiss that was as bold as yours;
A gift from gods to mortal worlds of men.
How can it be, they made a jewel that pours?
My ruler, lover, and friend for all of time:
You have been this, and more that can't be said.
In your embrace there's nothing that I dread.
We're born of earth and to the earth return,
And in between it's you who keeps me sane.
If love for you is sin then I shall burn,
For one mere drop of pleasure's worthy the pain.
     Seduction that pulls me in and keeps me close,
     Until, of course, I need another dose.

Nicole Landguth
Grade 12, La Jolla High
Poet-teacher: Gabriela Anaya Valdepeña
Teacher: Robin Visconti

BURRITO OF NATURE

My favorite food is bean and cheese burrito.
When you bite into it, it is squishy and tasty.
The moon is the tortilla and the beans are the soil from the
earth.
The cheese is strips of the sun.
It's hot and sometimes warm.
When I take a bite, I burst with joy like a volcano.
When I swallow, it feels like a rushing river down my throat.
When I eat Mexican food, it's great!

Caitlin Krol
Grade 3, St. Patrick's School
Poet-teacher: Jill Moses
Teacher: Jennifer Tappin

PEACH

Too hot to think
Only one haven
The orchard
Thick brown, soil
And tall trees ornamented
With warm juicy fruit
Red, Orange, Yellow, Purple
Swaying green leaves
Swirling around me
The best of all
The Porterville Paradise Peach
Warmed by the summer heat
It perches high
Waiting to be picked
Fuzzy, yellow-gold skin
Warm, sugary juice
Its sweet smell sticks to me
Soft—
Almost bursting in my hand.

Jared Addison Cotta
Grade 8, Lewis Middle
Poet-teacher: Jana Gardner
Teacher: Kathryn Dominique

How to Eat My Math

First you nibble the questions
Then you gobble the answer.
Be careful when you multiply,
It might become too much.
But when I divide, it is never enough.
And when I add to my tummy
It becomes a lot bigger
And sometimes it becomes too much bigger.
Then when I swallow subtraction
It becomes too small
But make sure that you rinse your number.
And make sure you blend your sevens.

Kaylee Nicole Turman
Grade 3, Tri-City Christian
Poet-teacher: Jill Moses
Teacher: Bobby Turman

A SPICY POEM

I am Tabasco
flavoring the world around me.
Yet I am also morning dew
unnoticed, and unknown to most.
But those who know me
Know that I can fly
without leaving the aground.
That I can swim
without getting wet.
That I can shine
without glowing.
That I can sing
without making a noise.
But it's different
for those who don't know me.
They say
He cannot fly
He cannot swim
Or shine
Or sing.
But unto all
I am Tabasco.
I flavor the world around me...

Alex Merryman
Grade 7, Mesa Verde Middle School
Poet-teacher: Glory Foster
Teacher: Daniel Fleming

I Will Never Live Without Rice

I believe God will only give you what you deserve
I believe love is only a word until you give it meaning
I believe there's someone who looks exactly like you
on a different planet acting as your reflection
I believe a rose has its thorns to protect its beauty
I don't believe in premarital sex
I will never visit a haunted house
I believe looks can be deceiving
Some guys lack knowledge when it comes
to deciphering a girl's way
I believe fame comes with a price
I don't believe in love at first sight
I will never live without rice
Friendship is a road with bumps along the way
Tardiness is laziness
You should take your shoes off before entering a home
I believe Berson should think twice about his actions
Rice Krispies really do talk
You find out who your real friends are in High School
Monsters don't live under your bed
I'll never starve myself to become sexy
And Trix aren't only for silly kids...

Rizalyn Vargas
Grade 9, Morse High
Poet-teacher: Glory Foster
Teacher: Carol Zupkas

ODE TO SUNFLOWER SEEDS

Thank you, thank you.
Your sun roasted
shell that cracks
like a gunshot across
the outback, chasing the
crunching of its pearl.
The seed
is the joy the pirates find
as you save
the captain from
all failure. You
saved my dad
from smoking.
Your delicious
pearl is like
a firefighter
who pulls my dad
from the hand of
smoke.

Jessi Hampton
Grade 5, St. Patrick's School
Poet-teacher: Jill Moses
Teacher: Anne Kramer

En el Centro de la Guitarra

En el centro de la guitarra
se mueven dedos delicados
con sonidos de agua
arrullando la linda mañana
acompañada de dulces voces
que parecen ángeles
volando entre las brisas...

In the Center of the Guitar

In the center of the guitar
delicate fingers move
with sounds of water
rocking the beautiful morning to sleep
accompanied by sweet voices
that look like angels
flying through the breeze. . .

Griselda Guadalupe Aguilar Polino
Age 15, Casa-Hogar Lirio de los Valles Tijuana
Poet-teacher: Francisco Bustos
Director: Sara Duña

POETRY IS ...

Poetry
is
pictures
in a
book,
the sweet
sound
of music.

Christina Thomas
Grade 3, Marshall Elementary
Poet-teacher: Jana Gardner
Teacher: Alicia Allen

ODE TO GOD

The grandmother puts spicy salsa
On the fruits of God. Everyone
Watches her. With all of the patience in
The world, she prepares the fruit
To go to the ones who want to live
With God's blessing.

ODA DE DIOS

La abuela le pone salsa picante
A las frutas de Dios. Todos la veen.
Con toda la paciencia del mundo
Prepara la fruta. Para irse la
A dar a todos los que queren vivir,
con la bendicion de Dios.

Alexis Sherman
Grade 5, San Diego Jewish Academy
Poet-teacher: Jill Moses
Teacher: Fran Miller

IMAGINARY ANGEL

I am the whistle of the wind
Blowing through the trees
I am the soft mellow chirping
Of winter's chickadees
I am the ghostly pirate ship
Sailing through seas of salt
I am the good friend sitting next to you
Who would like to share your malt
I swim through pools of water
Deep, clear and blue
I am the soft green of spring
Or winter's frosty hue
I am the raspberry sky
Releasing caramel rain
I am the curious thought
In the corner of your brain
I am everywhere and nowhere
Sometimes in between
I am the rose's pale petal
And the leaves of trees so green
I am the joys of life
So glorious and yellow
I am your imaginary angel
Stopping by to say, "Hello..."

Caitlin Crowley
Grade 7, Mesa Verde Middle School
Poet-teacher: Glory Foster
Teacher: Janet Helbock

"Christmas" by Abigail Rodriguez
Morse High

SESTINA FOR HEAVEN

As God floats in heaven,
way up in the air,
he awakens your eyes
so you can see the light.
Your mind is empty.
Thinking of nothing there, you lie

where angels also lie,
way up in heaven.
The world seems empty
with no fresh air.
God is there in the light
he keeps his eyes

on everyone's eyes.
In his eyes, angels lie
surrounded by light
in the depths of heaven,
in the holy air.

Heaven is empty
of earthly air, empty
of dark things. Angel eyes
are air, only air.
God is always awake, he lies
and stands in heaven,
on earth, everywhere with light.

God sheds light.
He is never empty.
He loves heaven.
Heaven relates his eyes.
Angels lie
in the shared air.

Power is air.
The air is light.
Angels lie.
in heaven, never empty
because of God's eyes,
bright in heaven.

God flies in the air, up in heaven,
awakens our eyes and brings light
to our world, empty of darkness, where we lie.

Tyler Maskiewicz
Grade 4, Spreckles Elementary
Poet-teacher: Gabriela Anaya Valdepeña
Teacher: Peggy Araiza

"Disaster" by Julie Charernsuk / Morse High

In The Middle Of Kandinsky

A sky as dark s gray midnight.
A purple snake in the ocean
sticking its tongue out at me.
Eyes that blink in the yellow plains of gold.
A sky-blue turtle shell, hiding from his prey.
A tiny temple of hot sunset colors.
A kite with funny facing, laughing at me.
A solar eclipse in the gold sky.
A tic-tac-toe board in the yellow grass.
Little hills in the ocean with baby fingers.
The ice mountain covered in green moss
in the middle of cool crazy colors.

Andrea Miller
Grade 4, Jerabek Elementary
Poet-teacher: Celia Sigmon
Teacher: Nancy Walters

I AM THE FIERY BREATH

I am the fiery breath of a dragon
the only silver scale on a snake
the ice cold skin of a serpent
the beautiful hair on a horse
I am the moon high in the sky
the glow of a star on Starry Night
the feathers of a dove
the down of a baby swan
I am the asteroid in outer space
the weight in the clouds at night
the wet dew on the green soft grass
the glitter on a picture frame
I am the eyes of a dark black cat
I am the trunk of a fever tree
I am the lead in the pencil you hold
I am the paper you hold in your hand
I am the poem that you are reading

Tatiana Kotas
Grade 4, Westwood Elementary
Poet-teacher: Jill Moses
Teacher: Andrea Barraugh

Honorable Mentions

"Moonlit Night" by Erica Skoglund / Mesa Verde Middle

HONORABLE MENTIONS

"Young Stallion with Father"
by Shelby Dinslage / Canyon View Elementary

Ada Harris Afterschool Program

Julia Hall, Silver Bubbles
Erika Mazza, *Owls*
Makenzie Stone, *War*

Aldea Infantil SOS Tijuana

Sandra Moreno Angues, *Mi Madre*
Jose Roberto Villalobos, *Mother, You Are the Sweater..*

Canyon View Elementary

Ian Cable, *The Feeling of Money*
Brianna Krenson, *The Gift of Giving*
Lisa Krieg, *The Memories of a River*
Nicole Love, *The Jubilant Kitchen*
Krista-Mae Ropa, *Existence of Tigers*
Matthew Schwartz, *Ode to the Amethyst*

Central Elementary

Ashley Jocelyn Covarrubias, *Como Ser La Nieve*
Jocelyne Eloy, *Grandma Whale*
Lucia Gama, *Grandma*
Valerie Gurrola, *My Mom's Hands*
Briana Majas, *I Am the Emotional Sun*
Gustavo Tovar, *Mystical Flute*
Crystal Del Valle, *Dreams of the Animals*
Cindy Gaytán, *Cold Salty Water*
Charlie Millar, *Cheetah and a Cat's Dream*

Del Mar Heights Elementary

Kevin Morgan, *Ode to a Computer*
Dan Savage, *My Backyard*
Maggie Scott, *The Petal*

Dingeman Elementary

Mike Bernardy, *Volcano of Might*
Austin Cole, *The Vibrant Sun*
Monica Hampton, *Drops of Heaven*
Jacob Ian Johanesen, *The Golden Firefly*
Kameron Kubis, *My Powerful Lightning Fingers*
Maggie Little, *A Great Gift*
Prithvi Undavalli, *Silent Night*
Victoria Unetic, *Wonderful Motions*
Cathy Zou, *The Holders of Dreams*

"Elements" by Matthew McCarthy
Mesa Verde Middle

Doyle Elementary

David Grey, *Volcano Mountain*
Landon Cummings, *We Light Fires*
Lucia Leoni, *Water Family*

El Toyon Elementary

Elioenay Alcade, *Music*
Reymond Bujanovsky, *Football*
Jodie Anne Gabriel, *The Bright Sun*

Farb Middle

Cassandra Fait, *In Silence*

Franklin Elementary

Ashley Compton, *The Magic of Poetry*

"Save the Pandas" by Lisa Nguyen / Standley Middle

"Love is Patient" by Katrina Gutierrez / Morse High

Greenfield Middle

Lynette Clayton, *Paradise*
Kylie Hensley, *Enlightened Midnight*
Brandi Hines, *Our Family Universe*
Tanya Hirmiz, *The Lady and the Four Phones*
Cody Horn, *The Crying Sun*
Carol Newland, *Glass of Water*
Jonathon Ramirez, *Maurice Boquet Playing Chamber Music*
Zack Raver, *Busy Buttons*
Chelsea Robertson, *Purple Fox*
Amber Rogers, *Scream*
Fenton Sue, *Memory's Persistence*
Douglas Winter, *Heaven's Gift: Wisteria*
Kelly Yost, *Spring Time*

Hawthorne Elementary

Priya Bisarya, *Ingredients for a Cheerful Soup*
Andrey Payne, *The Whispering Whistle*
Cleo Person, *Gods of Beautiful Poetry*
Channing Tullio, *Shadows of Hope*
Michael Wayne, *Beautiful New Beginnings*
Stefan Wendel, *The Salty Sea*

Jacumba Elementary

Drew Hancock, *What I Think About Black*
Laura Nuñez, *Grandpa*
Leilani Urbina, *Independent Blue*

Jerabek Elementary

Evan Critchlow, *Slithering Snake*
Darrell Day, *Crowned*
Bradley Furman, *Sunrise*
Meredith Gray, *Grandpa*
Marianne Linton, *Mostly About School*
Molly Merkin, *Brown Bag*
Morgan Robotta, *Garden Rainbow*
Cody Savage, *The Moon Is Sleeping*
Mary Simms, *Angela*
Kristina Tabar, *Oma*
Tara Thornton, *Midsummer Eve*
Alexandra Wolman, *Dancing Snowflakes*

Kimball Elementary

Kevin Ceron, *Sad Day*

"Where the Wild Things Are"
by Allura Hayes / Doyle Elementary

La Jolla Elementary

Sarah Delos Santos, *The Island of the Free Insects*
Erica Eisen, *Confused Sweet Pool*

"Sad Cow Disease" by Karl Asuncion / Morse High

La Jolla High

Noah Hy Brozinsky, *Gravity vs. the Pomeranian*
Ben Durwood, *Stopping by the Woods*

Las Palmas Elementary

Kreshelle Garcia, *Falling into a Pile of Snow*
Brianna Glass, *What I Can See*

Lewis Middle

Devyn J. Bullock, *Precious Moments Slipping Away*
Lauren Johnson, *What is Poetry?*
Ashley Marquez, *Hidden Within Me*

Lincoln Acres Elementary

Vincent Cadigal, *The Cowboy Hat*
Kimberly Guerrero, *Moon*
Steven Jacquez, *Rudolph's Red*
Jacob Pucci, *Nana*

Longfellow Middle

Krystal Reyes, *My Backyard of Knowledge*
Ariana Ronquillo, *My World*

Marshall Middle

Canna Dang, *The Forest of Dreams*
Martha Lopez, *Beautiful Ocean*
Helene Pham, *Magical Waterfall*
Sarah Sen, *I Am*
Sothun Touek, *My Cats, Angel and Lei Lei*

Mesa Verde Middle

Jessica Chang, *My Father's Hands*
Erica Crawford, *What You See*
Keri Downs, *Loneliness*
Mark Govea, *The Sound of a Million Words*
Charlotte Koczera, *Worker Ants*
Cody Walwick, *Who Am I?*

"The Inside Out Dalmation"
by Shireen Ashtari / Mesa Verde Middle

"A Snowy Day" by Megan Winslow
Canyon View Elementary

Morse High

Leizl C. Bergado, *Karate*
Andrea Bradley, *Jewel in the Desert*
Kenneth Chan, *The Flowing River*
Mark Dayrit, *Flawed Amethyst*
Richard Juliano, *Realm of Miracles*
Chau Mai, *The Unknown Truth*
Kristine Negado, *A Taste of Peace*
April Orsolino, *An Injured Heart*
Kenneth Panganiban, *A Necessary War*
Brian Pastran, *1,000 Eyes Watching Anger*
Renee Angeli Perez, *Fading Photographs*
Stefanie Quichocho-Rosario, *Green, Clumsy Broccoli Green*
Diana Quito, *Where the Orange Sun Rules*
Randall Allen Rivera, *Playing Video Games and Life's Games*
Daniel Smith, *God Made Me a Go-Kart*
David B. Smith, *Sir Turtle*
Jeffrey Topacio, *Static Saturday Nights and Square Balloons*
Christopher M. Whitley, *Sunflower Seeds, I Guess*

"Cranes" by Hochi Zuka / Doyle Elementary

Mueller Charter

Vianney Barraza, *Oda Á Tijuana*
Manuel Oswaldo Marquez, *Cuando Voy Á Tijuana*
Raul Perez, *En Tijuana*

New Horizons

Natalie Garcia, *The Wonder of My Grandpa*
Ronnell Miranda, *My Dad the King*
Romeo Valdez, Jr., *Mysterious Black*

Patrick Henry High

Braulio Lopez, *Courage, an Unsharpened Sword*

St. Patrick's School

Renier Cava, *I Like Food*
Sarah Connolly, *The Sparkler*
Anna Dornisch, *Go Inside My Brain*
Ashley Garcia, *I Am, I Am*
Trenton Gurley, *Soda Can*
Gioia Kabel, *What's in My Hands?*

Maya Le Espiritu, *Midnight Black and White*
Sarah Martin, *Empty*
Ryan E. Rees, *The War*
Keaton Riley, *I Am a Free Golden Spirit*
Chase Totoris, *No One Is Alike*

San Diego Jewish Academy

Lauren Bender, *Shooting Star*
Lee Brage, *Storm*
Jack Doshay, *Growing Greener*
Marila Lombrozo, *Who Will I Be When I Grow Up?*
Solomon Mizrachi, *Instead of Rain*
Irving Stone, *Ode to the Moon*
Robert Yedidsion, *Speak*

San Pasqual Union

Alyssa Brown, *Not a Rose*
Robyn Disher, *Shiny Stone*
Sami Marshall, *Obsidian's Secrets*
Jania Myers, *Ode to the Setting Sun*

San Diego Creative and Performing Arts

Danielle Catudio, *Golden Sunset*
Alexia Palladino, *Less Than Perfect*

"The Lonely Cobra" by Sothun Toeuk / Marshall Elementary

"Lost Turtle" by Kristina D. Marquez / Morse High

Southwest Middle

Yasmine Alcantara, *The Absence of Hatred*
Paola Arredondo, *My Baby Sister*
Adrian Brown, *Me*

Spreckles

Mason Betzenderfer, *Ode to Insulin*
Antigone Brickman, *Words*
Georgina Catzin, *A Friend*
Reese Fox, *The Yellow Sun*
Adilene Ortiz, *My Pencil*
Alexander Perdomo, *Wingless Angel*

Standley Middle

Troy Buchanan, *Electricity*
Sarah Miller, *The Winter Brings...*
Robert Phillips, *All Around Us, Lies*

Tri-City Christian

Mercedes Harvey, *Broccoli and Beef*

University City High

Kristina Kostenkova, *Earth*
Xiangyi Lin, *My Yellow Face*

Valley Vista Elementary

Brianna Adame, *Snowboard Lightning*
Brittney Greene, *The Pouncing Rainbow Cat*
Shanelle Dorn, *White Unicorn in the Wind*
Dirk Mendis, *Dad*
Diana Sanchez, *Lonely Planets*

Westwood Elementary

Lindsey Brewer, *Dancing With the Moon*
Victor Castro, *A Day In God's Shoes*
Melinda Chu, *Ode to Rose*
John Cooley, *Eraser vs. Lead*
Sayaka Inoue, *Future Bird*
Allison Refermat, *Ode to Night Sky*

"Bird in Flight" by Genevieve Nylen / Mesa Verde Middle